The Right Way to Keep Dogs

The Right Way to Keep Dogs

BY

R. C. G. HANCOCK, B.Sc., M.R.C.V.S.
(Formerly "Radio Vet." of the B.B.C.)

Illustrated by his daughter, Elaine Hancock

PAPERFRONTS
ELLIOT RIGHT WAY BOOKS
KINGSWOOD SURREY U.K.

Made and printed by Cox & Wyman Ltd, London, Reading and Fakenham

CONTENTS

To those Teachers

Who taught me to be
sceptical of the accepted

PREFACE

THE excuse for the production of this book is the need for a reliable, inexpensive handbook for dog lovers, covering adequately the diverse subjects that the average dog-loving amateur needs to keep his companion in the best of health.

The amateur who has been launched into keeping a dog on the lines laid down here should be able to maintain his pet in a healthy and happy state. He should be in a better position than most, if he wishes to extend his reading and doggy activities, to sift the wheat from the chaff when he turns to other sources for greater detail. For it must be acknowledged that much nonsense, morbid sentimentality and dangerous empiricism can be found in dog literature, resulting in faulty upbringing, dieting and unnecessary dosing with nauseating concoctions. This volume is based on the natural history of the species, drawing its conclusions from that enlarged common sense which a veterinary surgeon of long experience necessarily comes to possess if he has made good at his craft.

The facts are as accurate as my knowledge and reading can make them. The deductions from the facts must necessarily be subject to human error, and the pace of modern research has no mercy upon authors.

R.C.G.H.

CHAPTER I

THE NATURAL HISTORY OF THE DOG

IN my lectures and broadcasts, I have always found that if, from the outset, a beginner is told how an animal lives in its natural environment, before domestication comes upon its way of living, then many of the faults and errors of animal management can be avoided. So let us consider how the wild dog faces up to the problems of life.

Despite the assertions of behaviourists such as Lorenz, who divide dogs into two families, those predominantly wolfish in inheritance or those favouring the jackal temperament, and despite the fact that one suspects the early dingo-like ancestors of the dog were promiscuous in their acceptance of these foreigners as occasional mates, I prefer to think the Almighty created the prototype dog, even as He did the wolf and the jackal.

These ancestors were dingo-like creatures, about terrier size, with yellow-tan or black-and-tan coats as a basic colour in most instances. They hunted in packs by day or on moonlit nights and developed considerable cunning in combined operations to secure their prey. What is their prey can be judged accurately by a study of the life-history of the dog tapeworms, which have to pass a stage of their life-history encysted in the muscles of animals that are the normal diet of the dog family. And we find that the common tapeworms of the dog pass this intermediate resting stage in sheep, cattle, deer, antelopes, rabbits and fish.

IMPORTANCE OF DIET

While dogs are carrion eaters in the sense that they like their meat high, and have a good resistance to the putrefactive germs of flesh, observation has shown that the carnivores after a kill always immediately devour the liver and other intestinal organs, and drink the blood, but usually leave the flesh until later. And it is only recently that biochemists have shown that the liver is the repository of the vitamins of the body and that the traces of the various minerals essential to the body are obtained in greatest quantity from blood. The red cells of the blood are known to be rich in iron, for example. Another mineral vital to the skeletal frame, and in some areas deficient in the soil, is lime. The early dog, like his present-day descendant, needed a constant supply of this chemical, both in puppyhood and when adult. The bones of the prey are the source of supply of lime to the carnivore, whereas it is the lime from the soil, contained in grass and plant tissue, upon which grazing herbivores must rely.

So the dog is, by natural disposition a flesh-eating hunter. The very large size of the stomach, in relation to the animal and the rest of the digestive tube, indicates that he is capable of dealing with big meals at long intervals, rather than small but frequent feeds. In fact a dog does very well on only one meal a day. His gastric juice is exceptionally rich in hydrochloric acid and can rapidly soften bones. In the wild state, the ability of the less important intestine to digest cellulose is infinitesimal, whereas in the vegetarian horse it has to be an important function. This indicates that vegetable matter is of little or no value to the dog as diet, despite his well-known habit, when bilious, of eating grass stems as a preface to the act of vomiting. Again, the biochemists have revealed that the dog is almost unique in that he can synthesize in his body the all-important anti-scurvy vitamin C, of which fruit and vegetables are the indispensable source in the human.

So although dogs in domestication can adapt themselves to a cereal diet and may in some instances develop a passion for certain fruits, they are not primarily starch and sugar eaters. If they are to be kept on a staple diet of dog biscuit and bread, it is obvious that they must not only have access to a reasonable quantity of meat but of the vital content of fresh liver and offals, if they are not slowly to develop signs of one or other of what we call the deficiency diseases.

Everyone is familiar with the ineradicable instinct of the dog, prior to curling up for sleep, of scratching the floor or cushion on which he rests and then turning round and round in a circle before settling down. One can picture some shady spot in rank grass undergrowth, where this ritual softens the floor beneath and winds the long grass stems into a nest round his body. Unlike the fox and badger, the dog does not "go to earth" for his rest, but prefers to remain above ground and to make a shelter much as the hare does in its "form". One can draw the necessary inference in making a bed for the domestic pet.

Dogs hunt both by sight and scent, the wild dogs using either or both at need. In the wide desert areas, sight is the sense, whereas in dense jungle the nose must be guide to the quarry. And just as the ear of the dog will respond to a whistle of a wavelength above that capable of reception by the human ear, so too there seems little doubt that dogs employ a second sight, beyond the range of the human retina, that can sense the long-past passage of other animals and track their courses after ordinary body scents could not longer persist as guides. In no other way can one explain the uncanny tracking-down performances of the bloodhound along a cross-country route previously traversed days before by a criminal.

LOVE-LIFE AND BREEDING

The love-life of dogs is worth study by those who breed them. The application of first principles has led, in my own experience, to fertility and large litters, where no litters or very small ones were the rule before my advice was sought. Normally the bitch comes "on heat" twice a year for three weeks, in spring and autumn. For the rest of the year she is of no interest to the male. In no species has Nature shown greater care in ensuring that there shall be the maximum fertility of the greatest number of bitches in the pack.

For the first week of her heat, the bitch will not consent

Afghan Hound

to consummate the act of mating. She is strongly attractive during this wooing period to all the males of the pack, who follow her in a hopeful procession, fighting among themselves from time to time, to settle the primacy of approach. The result is that by the second week, when the bitch allows mating to take place, she has gone through a process of strenuous wooing, so that the ovaries have been stimulated to shed a large number of eggs into the womb, there to await fertilization. Also, the first male to mate with her and therefore to have the first likelihood of fertilizing her eggs, has done so by reason of his superior physical power over the remainder of the males of the pack. Further, after this mating the bitch remains promiscuous in her acceptance, and when the prime mate has had his way, the second most dominant male will take his place, and so on down the scale of authority. Thus fertilization of the waiting eggs is ensured by every possible means and to a degree of certainty rare in mammals.

Only those familiar with the breeding technique of the present-day pedigree breeder will know how far their methods negative this natural certainty. The bitch is kept shut up during the week where she should be the object of constant wooing and stimulus by the male. On the day she is adjudged ready for the mating, she is taken and held, often muzzled, while the precious stud dog, lest he be injured, is carefully lifted into position. Under these conditions, with no love-making precedent to the act, both sexes are indolent in performance, eggs are few in number and the male seed poor in quality or quantity. In many cases, the "tying" of the dog to the bitch is not effected because of this sexual indolence. No wonder the resulting litter is small or non-existent. The curious thing is that though bitches snap at the dog with every appearance of ferocity, I have yet to meet the veterinary surgeon who has treated an injury sustained by a dog in his attempts to mate the bitch. Injuries inflicted by rival males on each other are, of course, common. So the owner of the pedigree dog would do well to let visiting bitches have as much wooing as possible. Let them have the run of a paddock or garden, and let the mating act occur as and when feeling dictates, and the resulting litters will be more satisfactory.

From what has just been said, it is obvious that a virgin bitch is an impossibility in a state of nature. So the oft asked question, "Should my bitch have an occasional litter for the good of her health?" would seem to require an affirmative answer.

Whelping

Another primal instinct that requires understanding by the owner of a bitch concerns the act of whelping. I have always urged that, if the arrival of the pups is to be as rapid as it should be, in even the artificial distorted lap-dog breeds, the strong instinct to hide away and be alone at such a time must be respected and, if need be with the pampered pet, enforced. The watched bitch in the act of parturition will hold up her pains again and again if well-meaning owners persist in sitting with the mother throughout the whelping. I have often arrived with the "black bag" and found that the only intervention necessary is to inveigle the attendant away for an hour. Only in this way can one demonstrate how rapid the birth of six or more puppies can be under conditions of darkness and seclusion.

Reversion to Wild State

One of the things the dog owner wants to learn from this chapter is that in times of stress, such as in illness, during parturition, following on injury or accident, all animals become for the time being wild animals, in the sense that their reaction to humans will be that of their wild forbears, rather than the superimposed manners of domestication. This feral (wild) reversion must be expected and allowed for in one's calculations and attitude to the pet dog. Again, let half a dozen dogs get together on the village green and one can almost see the ancient ancestral pack instinct rise up. In a few moments the group is away, and within a few hours a flock of pregnant ewes has been brought to a sorry state, with great loss to the farmer, not only in mauled, wounded and over-galloped sheep, but in abortions. One cannot blame the individuals of the hunting pack. It is an inevitable reversion to the wild where two or three are gathered together.

Enough has been said perhaps to justify basing one's judgment in future chapters upon the first principles that can be learned from a study of the dog in its natural state and surroundings.

Alsatian

POINTS OF THE DOG

1	Stop	7	Feather
2	Flews	8	Breeching
3	Muzzle	9	Hock
4	Occiput	10	Stifle
5	Loins	11	Elbow
6	Tail, Stern or Flag	12	Pastern

13 Brisket

GLOSSARY OF TERMS

Bat Ear: An erect ear.

Blaze: A white marking up the face.

Breeching: Feathering, or long hair, at the back of the legs above the hocks.

Brush: A bushy tail, e.g. in the Collie.

Butterfly Nose: A parti-coloured nose.

Button Ears: Ears in which the tips fall forward and almost cover the inside.

Cat Feet: Rounded and practically circular feet, with well-arched toes.

Chop: Loose, hanging upper lips. Flews.

Cobby: Thick-set and compact.

Couplings: That part of the body between the shoulders and the hips.

Cow Hocks: Hocks which point inwards towards each other.

Dew Claw: The extra claw above the foot, usually removed.

Dewlap: The loose skin at the throat.

Dish Face: A hollowed face, showing a concave line in profile.

Docked: With the tail shortened.

Dome: The raised part between the ears at the junction of the head and neck.

Dudley Nose: A pink or flesh nose.

Feather: Long hair on the legs, tail or ears.

Flag: A Setter's tail.

Flews: Loose, hanging upper lips. Chop.

Goose-rumped: A sloping rump.

Hare Foot: A narrow, long, hare-like foot.

Harlequin: A white coat with dark patches (as Harlequin Great Dane).

Hound Colours: Black-and-white; black, tan-and-white; pied.

Level Mouth: Even mouth; upper and lower teeth meeting.

Occiput: The peak or dome of the skull.

Otter Tail: A round tail.

Overshot: The upper jaw projecting over the lower. Swine-chopped; pig-jawed; parrot-mouthed.

Parti-coloured: White with darker patches.

Peak: The occiput.

Pig-Jaw: Overshot.

Prick Ears: Erect ears.

Puppy: Under Kennel Club Rules, an animal not over 12 months old.

Roach Back: A back curving upward at the loins, as in the Whippet. Wheel Back.

Roan: A mixture of colours and white; the predominating colour gives the name, thus, blue roan.

Rose Ears: Ears which curl inwards and then out and backwards.

Smut: A whole colour with a black muzzle or face.

Tulip Ears: Erect ears with the tips bending forward.

Undershot: With the lower jaw projecting beyond the upper, as in the Bulldog.

Wall-eyed: An eye without pigment in the iris.

Whole Colour: One body colour.

CHAPTER II

CHOOSING YOUR DOG

WHEN it comes to keeping dogs for some special reason, such as shooting, rabbiting with ferrets, ratting, watching the house, guarding sheep, obviously one will go to one of the breeds that for generations have been used for these special functions. The natural aptitude of a breed accustomed for centuries to one specific purpose has resulted in a hereditary performance so high in some instances that training for the task is reduced to almost nothing. Many a Sheepdog puppy, shown a flock for the first time, performs most of the evolutions of shepherding without instruction. To obtain the same result with a Fox Terrier or a Greyhound might take years of teaching, and in a large proportion of instances would be unsuccessful. The choice is therefore a narrow one and needs little or no exposition at this stage.

It is in the choice of a pet and companion where guidance may be of help. Veterinary surgeons are constantly asked to advise their clients. Some psychological insight is required here, as well as a knowledge of the home and the people in it. For instance, if the enquirer is a Hollywood lovely, she probably has something unique, spectacular, and horribly expensive already present in her subconscious. Visions of Borzois, Deerhounds, or, at the other extreme, Pekinese and Maltese Terriers, must be catered for. With the more mundane owner of moderate means, it would be foolish to recommend a Great Dane or Bull Mastiff to dwell in a three-room London flat.

In these days, price is undoubtedly a ruling factor. The reasonably pedigreed puppy of any breed, which in 1939 could be obtained within a five pound note, may well cost five to ten times this amount today. Bitches cost more than the price of the male, as a rule. If one is content with a puppy which is the result of an accidental misalliance, the cost of course is much less and may sometimes be only a couple of pounds. In making such purchases, try to ascertain the parentage. I have seen a little ball of fluff alleged to be a Pekinese grow into something like a St. Bernard, to the dismay of its owner, through neglect of this precaution.

The temperaments of the parents count for a good deal in mongrel crosses. Thus, the Alsatian or Sheepdog parent can bring in a sly viciousness, or a thieving propensity. Spaniel-Terrier crosses are generally satisfactory and usually two docile parents of the domestic varieties produce good-mannered offspring. But it is wrong to think that the mongrel has any advantage over the pure-breed in resistance to disease. Apart from the good constitution that the introduction of new blood brings, as in outcrosses used sometimes by pedigree breeders, the mongrel is just as prone to die of distemper or any other doggy disease as is his pedigreed relation.

A word of warning about that tragic multitude of unwanted dogs of uncertain forbears. Any dog picked off the streets and taken to a dogs' home is not only fertile ground, by reason of fear and hunger, for virus and bacterial invasion, but also is more likely to encounter these lethal foes in the dogs' shelter than anywhere else. Ideally every stray dog should have a kennel and run to himself but in dogs' homes they are usually put with some twenty or thirty others. In that number of strays there is bound to be one or more "carriers" of some infective state ranging in bulk from the ultra-microscopic virus to the visible and demonstrable flea.

Dogs for the Home

Many of the specialized breeds make excellent pets and the smaller-sized ones are particularly suitable for town life. The Spaniel has long been a favourite, apart from his aptitude for work with the gun. In addition to intelligence and good temper, he is a very gay creature, always cheerful and affectionate. A good eater, he often runs to middle-age spread, a tendency that is aided by his ingratiating ways when food is about, and a disposition of this breed to thyroid deficiency, which even with care in diet leads to great obesity.

Basenji

The Retrievers are also of delightful temperament and with Spaniels and the Boxer are probably three of the best breeds to have when young children are about. They stand endless mauling and torment from the youngsters without loss of temper and retaliation. The Terriers are all game, pugnacious and sporting in their outlook on life. Their true métier is out of doors in the country, though many have been adapted to life in towns. The English, Scottish and Irish Terriers all have their devoted adherents; and one should not forget the Sealyham, a breed evolved in the last two generations and intended by its originator to go to earth for fox or badger. The blue-coated Bedlington, though rather a "scrapper", is popular, as is the Border Terrier.

Of the more decorative fancy breeds, there are many varieties. They are good little pals and many, like the Pekes and Yorkshire Terriers, are exceedingly game and cheeky and not at all the pampered lapdog in their outlook upon life. I have always had rather a weakness for Griffons. Whether smooth or rough-coated, they are born comedians and exceedingly faithful to their owner.

But the field of choice is wide. The Kennel Club grants full recognition to round about one hundred different breeds. Having settled the price, the breed of choice, the size to fit in with the home and the type of temperament likely, as indicated by the parentage, all should be well.

BUYING THE DOG

Then comes the question: where to obtain the dog? Here there can be many pitfalls. "Let the buyer beware" applies to dogs almost to the same degree as it does to horse-dealing. While in the towns there are pet shops and great stores that can be relied upon for fair treatment and that take every precaution against their charges contracting disease while on the premises, yet there are too many establishments whose sole interest is to sell their wares and who subsequently repudiate all responsibility for what may happen afterwards to their charges. The recently or barely weaned puppy is always a good sales proposition. Women and children are attracted to these little waifs. Yet the mortality in these babes is so high that one wishes there could be some control over the age at which they may be exposed for sale in shop windows. Even with the greatest care in disinfection of premises, the employment of preventive inoculations and avoidance of overcrowding, carriers of disease get into and infect these premises from time to time.

All veterinary surgeons, particularly around Christmas

time, get a crop of indignant new owners bringing in the recently purchased puppy and find the latter affected with maybe distemper, fleas, lice, ringworm, mange, worms or digestive upsets. And in the case of distemper, it can often be declared that the puppy has had it for a period that makes it beyond doubt that it had the disease at the time of sale. Too often, on returning to the shop, the vendor is inflexible and refuses to do anything about it. It is good that at last Parliament, in the Pets Shop Act, has provided that these too often disreputable establishments shall have periodical inspection by the Local Authority. The Pet Trade Association in conjunction with the B.S.A.V.A. grants a diploma to members who have passed the Association's examination in the keeping of animals under hygenic and suitable conditions. This diploma will be displayed in the best pet shops.

In the working-class districts of London and other towns, there often exist kerbside markets where puppies and illicitly acquired dogs of value can be obtained cheaply. So far as the puppies are concerned, great cruelty is involved in this traffic. These pathetic little babes are picked up by a dealer for a song, and are kept in dark insanitary backyard sheds, where they become infected with parasites, skin disease or germs such as distemper. Their food is usually so unsuitable that within a day or two they become affected with intestinal troubles.

The result is that a large proportion of them fall ill a few days after purchase and mortality is high. I made investigations into this traffic and found, after looking into the records of a dozen poor persons' Clinics in the London area, that of every hundred puppies brought for treatment and acquired by this means, often at outrageously high prices, twenty-five had to be destroyed outright as beyond treatment and half of the remainder eventually died or had to be destroyed. This enquiry, over a year's figures, only covered twelve Clinics and did not cover the surgeries of veterinary surgeons, yet it involved thousands of animals. Therefore, if the whole of Great Britain is included, it is obvious that action is urgently needed to control this traffic. I have thought it well to give some details of this, in order that the reader may avoid the temptation to acquire a puppy from such a source. As to the residue of stolen dogs obtainable in such street markets, no comment is needed as to the folly of obtaining a dog in such circumstances.

Having taken care to select a reputable source, and completed purchase, it is a cheap insurance to let your veterinary surgeon run the rule over the animal, the same day if possible. It is wise to let the vendor know that you intend doing this. I have heard of instances, when this intention was announced, of the vendor immediately refusing sale—a clear indication he has something to hide as to the health of his animals. If the veterinary surgeon is satisfied, there is not much to worry about. But if, as happens too often, he finds signs of incipient disease, obtain a certificate to that effect, go straight back to the vendor and either demand your money back, agree to repurchase as soon as the animal is certified as cured, or make some mutually agreeable arrangement that safeguards you from total loss by disease. Many kennels will take back the animal and offer another in exchange. This may be fair in some circumstances, but in others—say, where distemper exists obviously on the premises—it would be unwise to assent without safeguards.

And when, after purchase, you do find something wrong, do not delay getting professional advice, in the mistaken belief that it may be nothing serious and the puppy may be all right tomorrow. Far too often, because of this delay in getting veterinary advice and a certificate, the vendor is able to plead that the illness must have started after purchase; and owing to the lapse of time, it becomes impossible for veterinary evidence to carry the weight it should in settling disputes. The result is that the buyer not only pays for the animal, but veterinary as well as legal fees, if he seeks redress through the Courts, and is left with no dog in the end if the latter dies or has to be destroyed.

Always, if possible, have a look round the place where the intended pet comes from. See the animals on the premises, if it is a breeding or boarding establishment. Are they well looked after? Do the buildings, as you enter them, smell wholesome? Are the beds that the dogs rest

Basset Hound

on clean? Look around the food shed and make enquiries about the diet. Watch the dogs in the runs. Are they happy and active, in good condition; or do they look wretched, hungry, even cowed? A lot of scratching and evidence of bare patches on the skin indicate parasites— a sure sign of bad hygiene and faulty management. There is no excuse for fleas, lice, mange or ringworm in a kennel in these days. If many of the animals appear listless and inclined to lie up in their beds, despite the arrival of visitors, and coughs and sneezes are heard, or the eyes and nostrils show evidence of catarrhal discharge, you can be pretty sure distemper is present. Anyone who offers a dog for sale under such circumstances can only be doing so for one reason—in the hope of selling off apparently healthy stock while the going is still good, before signs of disease spread further among his stock.

Pedigrees are often worth no more than the paper they are written on and are produced by unscrupulous dealers in order to put up the price of an inferior animal. On the other hand, if breeding is envisaged, a genuine pedigree can be very useful when puppies come to be sold later. So take every step to ensure that they are both genuine and accurate and are signed by the breeder, together with the address.

These precautions and dangers of course beset the urban purchaser far more than the dweller in the country. The latter probably knows the seller, or can acquire the knowledge from neighbours. Moreover, purchase from a non-professional source is far less likely to result in disease or dissatisfaction over the purchase in country districts.

Apart from disease, some time after purchase, undesirable character traits may show themselves. Some of these may be due to wrong handling on the part of the owner. Others are inherited characteristics, and when they involve savage attacks on members of the family, inveterate stealing, sheep or poultry chasing, it is often wiser to cut the sentimental attachment at once and have the animal put away. The alternative, within my own experience, may not only be medical and legal costs, but maiming for life, where sentimentality has been allowed to take the place of sentiment.

One must realize that there are morons and crooks in the world of dogs as well as in that of mankind. It can be extremely difficult, particularly when an affection has been created between man (or more often woman) and dog, to make the owner see the risks run by holding on to these dangerous animals. Where there are children in the family, it is criminal. Yet every veterinary surgeon has seen instances of this, has failed in his pleading to get the animal removed, and has had the sorrow of seeing the results of this selfishness later on, when damage has been done.

It should be remembered that original sin, with a tendency to vice, advanced forms of mischief, disobedience, thieving, are not necessarily incurable, or indications of hopeless criminal tendency. Much can be done by training and discipline to rectify these incipient faults in a puppy, up to the first year of life. But in the adult there is little hope of cure. That is one good reason for (as a rule) not acquiring an adult dog. The puppy that grows up with the family can usually be moulded to the heart's desire, whereas the adult has habits fixed and virtually unalterable by the time he enters his second year of life. In any case, even in the puppy, intolerance of reasonable chastisement, with a tendency to bite, resent discipline and take revenge, should be regarded as a danger signal and as probably not worth attempting to cure. In puppies of large breeds, such as Alsatians or the great Hounds, it may mean that the adult is going to be potentially capable of *manslaughter*; and with these large breeds, such types should be ruthlessly eliminated.

After a general look round at the environment of your prospective pet and satisfying yourself on the points I have enumerated, you may concentrate on the animal of choice. If unweaned, there will be a chance of seeing its dam and the rest of the family—a great help in assessing vigour and the ultimate appearance of the puppy when adult. Note the manners of the dam, whether she is affectionate or apprehensive. Pick your puppy up and assure yourself it is in good bodily condition, for a heavy coat can often camouflage an undernourished skinny frame. The eyes should be bright and the limbs straight. Rickets, though much less common than it used to be, still occurs and any suggestion of curvature of the long bones of the limbs should awaken suspicion.

It is wise, if told that the puppy is weaned and able to feed itself, to see it take food. This assures one not only that the puppy has learned to feed itself, but that it has or has not an appetite for food. The droppings in the run can be a guide. The motions should be firm. Diarrhoea is often due to threadworms, though these are not always passed with each motion and may not therefore be visible. But the existence of diarrhoea should be commented upon and purchase delayed until the owner has found the cause and dealt with it. Part the hair and look for signs of irritation, particularly behind the ears and elbows and at the root of the tail. The presence of fleas is indicated more often by the presence of flea dirt in the coat. This looks like small accumulations of cigarette ash between the hairs close to the skin and will be found more certainly than the extremely mobile dog flea. The dog louse can be detected by little ivory specks the size of a pin's head, generally adherent to the skin in the region of the ears and rump. Mange (scabies) leads to an eruption of little spots inside the forelimbs and thighs, though later the head and body become invaded as well. There is in this disease intense irritation, with frequent scratching. If untreated, the animal loses sleep and becomes thin from lack of rest.

None of these skin diseases, with the possible exception of ringworm, need be the cause of rejection and refusal to purchase. But obviously one must decline to buy until the owner's veterinary surgeon certifies that the condition is cured. If you have any doubts, offer to send a veterinary surgeon of your choice to see the puppy on the breeder's premises. Reputable breeders who value their good name will make no objection to this course. They will not want you to take the pup for examination because of the traumatic effect of the animal should you return it, and the risk of it picking up more infection. Reputable breeders do not let puppies go on approval.

LIST OF BREEDS AND PURPOSES

I give below a list of the principal breeds recognized by the Kennel Club, with a few descriptive words on each.

AFGHAN HOUND. A dog of the greyhound type used for hunting in Afghanistan. Not an easy dog, in character or coat care, and only for the really dedicated, family with plenty of time to spare.

AIREDALE TERRIER. The largest of the British Terriers. Stands about 23 ins. tall, a good guard and vermin killer.

ALASKAN MALAMUTE. Sled dog from the Arctic. Very powerful and rather strong willed. Not for the novice owner. Weight about 100 lbs.

ALSATIAN. (German Shepherd Dog.) Intelligent and a good guard, needs firm handling and to come from stock with good temperament. See the sire and dam if you can. Could you live with them?

AMERICAN COCKER SPANIEL. Has much longer fringes than the English version, and requires a great deal of grooming.

AUSTRALIAN TERRIER. Rather like a large Yorkshire Terrier, weighs about 14 lbs. A bold and game family pet.

BASENJI. Descended from the Ancient Dogs of Egypt, and brought here from the Congo. Called the barkless dog, but by no means silent, they howl when necessary. Weight around 25 lbs., smooth coated.

BASSET HOUND. A hunting dog, low built, weighing about 50 lbs. Pleasant temperament, but needs a lot of exercise.

BEAGLE. Bred to hunt the hare by scent. A nice hound, easy to do with, but requires a strong fence to keep him in. He was bred to go, and he will . . . all day.

BEARDED COLLIE. A long-haired, working sheepdog. Good tempered, and medium size.

BEDLINGTON TERRIER. A woolly coat that needs trimming but does not shed hair. Great ratters, and fond of fight within the pack. Quiet disposition with the family.

BLOODHOUND. A very big dog on short legs. Weight some 100 lbs. bred to hunt, and requires a lot of exercise and control. Has some feeding problems. Not for the novice owner.

BORDER TERRIER. The hunt terrier. Game, tough and active. Weighs 15 lbs.

BORZOI. The Russian Wolfhound. Very elegant and beautiful. A specialist's dog, not for the rough and tumble of family life.

BOSTON TERRIER. An American gentleman, cross between the English Bulldog and the Bull Terrier. Weighs 25 lbs., great fun to own. Good temperament.

BOXER. The clown of the dog world. A good guard, a great playmate for children, inclined to be obstinate and demanding of human company. Weighs 65 lb. and throws it all at you!

BRIARD. The French Sheepdog. Long coat, a charming gentle dog. Quite large.

BULLDOG. The one everyone knows. Kind, courageous, slow to anger. The bitches are not easy to breed from, and as a breed they are not long lived.

BULLMASTIFF. The Mastiff/Bulldog cross, bred to protect gamekeepers. 130 lbs. of good-tempered magnificence. You need money and space to own this one, but he is a wonderful animal in the right conditions.

BULL TERRIER. Great fellas, if you like their looks. The ideal, brave housedog, and good with children. Weight 35 lbs. Miniatures, height about 14 ins.

CAIRN TERRIER. Tough, pleasant and active little dog. Daily grooming and exercise.

CARDIGAN WELSH CORGI. Heavier than his better known brother the Pembroke, he has a long bushy tail. Weight 26 lbs.

CAVALIER KING CHARLES SPANIEL. The largest toy breed. Glamorous, easy to live with, always cheerful. When in the country, quickly reverts to real hunting spaniel behaviour. Weight, 18–20 lbs.

CHIHUAHUA. A tiny mite, much stronger and more independent than he looks. Long and smooth coat varieties, both weighing not more than 6 lbs. Will fit the smallest flat and mini car.

CHINESE CRESTED. A tiny dog, almost hairless apart from a plume on head, feet and tail. Very loving.

CHOW CHOW. A proud and dignified Chinese gentleman, somewhat aloof to strangers, wonderful with his own family.

CLUMBER SPANIEL. A heavy gun dog, with a thick white coat. Weight 70 lbs. Not very numerous now.

COCKER SPANIEL. Deservedly, always very popular, a charming, energetic dog, with eyes that melt your good intentions. Need not suffer from ear trouble if you keep him clean.

DACHSHUND. Comes in two sizes, Standard at 20 lbs., Miniatures at 10 lbs., and three coats, smooth, wire and long-haired. They all make good pets, and sporting dogs.

DALMATIAN. The unmistakable horse carriage spotted dog, liver or black spots. Bred to cover long distances with ease, he still needs a great deal of free exercise.

DANDIE DINMONT TERRIER. A small and ancient Scottish breed, a faithful friend of the family.

DEERHOUND. 30 ins. tall, weight 100 lbs., a lot of dog under a rough grey coat. Gentle and yet still sporting, but not for suburban life.

DOBERMANN. A guard and police dog who needs firm handling and training. Not to be lightly taken on.

ELKHOUND. A hardy Norwegian dog with a thick coat, weight some 50 lbs. Thrives in cold conditions, needs firm handling.

ENGLISH SETTER. A big and beautiful gun dog, for the country.

ENGLISH SPRINGER SPANIEL. Wonderful at his work of hunting and bringing back game. Another who should work to be in his right element.

ENGLISH TOY TERRIER. Used to be called a black-and-tan. Tiny dog, weight 6–8 lbs., smooth coated, can be kept anywhere. A mite noisy.

FINNISH SPITZ. He looks like a fox, he was the hunting companion of Finland many hundreds of years ago. Very beautiful in his red coat and plumy tail.

FOX TERRIER. Smooth or wirehaired. Very popular terriers who are wonderful ratters.

FRENCH BULLDOG. Smooth coated, amusing, squashy face and large "bat" ears. Great fun to own, an ideal town dog. Weight 25 lbs.

GERMAN SHORTHAIRED POINTER. Smooth coated gun dog, very smart indeed. Wants some work to keep him happy.

GOLDEN RETRIEVER. Another beautiful long-coated gun dog, perfect with children, must have his exercise.

GORDON SETTER. A handsome balanced gun dog in black-and-tan rig-out. Needs the country.

GREAT DANE. 120 lbs. of gentle giant. Can reach your highest shelf. Loves to go out with horses across country, not just down to the pillar box.

GREYHOUND. Gentle and very restful pet, a poem to watch when he is moving flat out. A liability if you have to exercise in town parks, as he will chase cats and small dogs.

GRIFFON BRUXELLOIS. Like a little monkey, in looks and ways. Very clever. Weight about 8 lbs.

GROENENDAEL. The Belgian Sheepdog. A black coat. A friendly dog who makes a sensible guard.

IBIZAN HOUND. A smart prick eared dog in a rich red coat. A big bark, and he does not bite.

IRISH SETTER. So beautiful, affectionate and gentle, a wonderful gun dog who should have a job to do to keep him happy.

IRISH TERRIER. A true terrier with a wiry coat that needs trimming. Weight 25 lbs.

IRISH WATER SPANIEL. It would be cruel to keep him as a town pet. His curly coat was made for a swim suit, a wonderful dog for a shooting man.

IRISH WOLFHOUND. Very large, very aristocratic, a dog that demands a baronial hall and a stable. Don't buy him as a status symbol.

ITALIAN GREYHOUND. A drawing room edition of the greyhound, weighs about 8 lbs. and looks fragile, feels the cold. Not a dog for a rough and tumble family.

JAPANESE CHIN. A toy spaniel, very glamorous.

KEESHOND. The Dutch barge dog. Not a big dog underneath an enormous coat and a plumed tail. A great guard, very good with children.

KERRY BLUE TERRIER. A mid size terrier, weight 35 lbs. Needs firm handling as he likes to have a go.

KING CHARLES SPANIEL. Flat-faced toy breed, smaller and not so hardy as his cousin the Cavalier. A gentle pet.

LAKELAND TERRIER. Used for bolting foxes, a true terrier type in black-and-tan.

LHASA ASPOS. From Tibet, a long coated, very attractive dog, becoming more and more popular as a pet. Said to be long lived as dogs go.

MALTESE. So white and beautiful, a dog that needs to have daily grooming to look his best. Don't buy one unless you have the time to give to him.

MANCHESTER TERRIER. Hardy, tough, smooth-coated in black and tan. A good all-purpose dog.

MAREMMA. The Italian Sheepdog, with a long white coat. Very devoted guard dog.

MASTIFF. Ancient and enormous. Weighing perhaps 170 lbs. For the very special owner only.

MINIATURE PINSCHER. Lively little toy dog, an excellent pet.

NEWFOUNDLAND. Webbed feet, and water resistant double coat, he was made for swimming, and loves rescuing children from water. Makes a wonderful nanny for the right home with space.

NORFOLK TERRIER. Hardy little terrier, height 10 ins. His cousin the Norwich Terrier is the same, but with pricked ears.

Norwegian Buhund. Medium-sized dog, very nice family pet.

Old English Sheepdog. The Bobtail. Long, long coat that even covers his gentle eyes. Must have a lot of grooming, and does not thrive in central heating.

Papillon. The toy dog with butterfly ears. Gentle and charming companion.

Pekinese. Tougher, more obstinate than their size would indicate. Great for country or town in larger sizes. The very tiny ones, almost noseless, are rather specialist pets.

Pembroke Welsh Corgi. Made famous as royal pets, he has come a long way from his origin as a Welsh cattle dog. Makes a good family dog.

Pointer. A smart dog for the shooting man. He should have some work to do.

Pomeranian. Tiny, alert toy dog of some 5 lbs. Thick coat and plumed tail. Needs grooming well to look good. Amazing stamina for his size.

Poodle. Three sizes; standard, miniature and toy. All have huge coats which do not shed hair, but need regular clipping which can come expensive. An intelligent breed, for adults rather than children. A poodle is quite willing to rough it a bit, it is a pity he has been commercially exploited with accessories. Long lived as dogs go.

Pug. Unmistakable toy dog, full of fun.

Pyrenean Mountain Dog. Huge white-coated dog, weighing 150 lbs., or so. Nice tempered and good guards, but not suitable for a small home.

Retriever. The labrador; black, chocolate or yellow. An obliging, obedient, easy dog.

Alsation. Some keep as guard dogs.
Some can be very fierce.

There is also the flat-coated retriever, and the curly coated. All great workers.

ROTTWEILER. Continental police dog, strong, and intelligent. Needs training, but then is a joy to own. A black-and-tan short coat.

ROUGH COLLIE. A "Lassie" dog. Beloved of many families. His cousin the Smooth Collie is just as nice, not quite so glamorous.

ST. BERNARD. Enormous heavyweight dog in a big coat. Suffers in the heat and hot rooms. For the specialist only.

SALUKI. A graceful and ancient desert breed, very fast, and not inclined to stop once he has got going. You must have safe exercising ground.

SAMOYED. A white dog with a big coat, needs regular attention, to look his best. Weighs some 50 lbs.

SCHIPPERKE. The Belgian barge dog. Black mostly, some champagne and cream. Make smart little pets, weighing about 15 lbs.

SCHNAUZER. Three sizes; giant, standard and miniature. Originally cattle dogs in Germany. Great guards.

SCOTTISH TERRIER. Always popular, a very suitable family pet.

SEALYHAM TERRIER. Low-slung white dog, who does require a little time spent on his coat. Good with children.

SHETLAND SHEEPDOG. The "Sheltie". A small edition of the rough collie, with a rather sharp bark. Very popular pet.

SHIH TZU. Another from Tibet, with a very long coat. Devoted to his owners, always ready for a game. Excellent for children.

SKYE TERRIER. 25 lbs. of terrier with a mind of its own. Coat needs a lot of work.

STAFFORDSHIRE BULL TERRIER. Packed full of muscle, he needs strong and sensible handling. A lovely nature at home, he does like to sort out his fellow canines.

SUSSEX SPANIEL. Sturdy, heavy dog in liver colour. Deserves to be worked. Not very many about.

TIBETAN SPANIEL. Reminiscent of a pekinese, but with longer nose and legs. A very pleasant pet.

TIBETAN TERRIER. Like a small bob-tailed sheepdog. Getting very popular.

WEIMARANER. The "grey ghost" dog of unbelievably beautiful colour, yellowy eyes with a changing expression. A police and gun dog to be proud of, when properly trained.

WELSH SPRINGER SPANIEL. Handsome, useful dog in a red and white coat which does not require much attention. Weight 40 lbs.

WELSH TERRIER. Like a wire fox terrier, but in black and tan.

WEST HIGHLAND WHITE TERRIER. Very attractive, smart little dog in a harsh white coat. A good fellow to have.

WHIPPET. A small greyhound, quick and active. Devoted to owners.

YORKSHIRE TERRIER. A grand, game little dog that can stand pampering but does not need it. Long silky glossy coat that needs a lot of work to keep in show condition. Weight 6 lbs.

CHAPTER III

DIETETICS

FROM what has been said in the first chapter, in the consideration of the natural history of the dog before man interfered with his habits, it has to be conceded that he is a flesh-eating animal. Having said so much, one is bound to admit that the dog shows great adaptability in his power of deriving nourishment from foodstuffs not primarily designed for his digestive organs. Under the influence of domestication and of circumstances in times of privation, he has become virtually omnivorous, or, put less gracefully, a scavenger.

His teeth are the teeth of a flesh eater, designed not for the leisurely mastication of the starch and cellulose feeder, but for tearing and ripping the flesh from the bones and getting the meal quickly into its first digestive chamber, the stomach. The alkaline saliva, unlike our own, does not contain the starch-digesting ferment, ptyalin. So the anxiety of the novice on observing the indecent haste with which his or her pet bolts each and every meal is unnecessary. It may be mentioned that the invariable desire for food whenever available is another primal urge to gorge while the going is good and so lay by, as far as is practicable, for the hypothetical rainy day. Put in another way, the deduction is that because the dog appears hungry under the luxurious regime of home-life with humans, this begging for titbits and the giving of snacks between meals is not to be pandered to, unless one aims at making the pet a liverish, prematurely-aged dyspeptic half-way through life.

UNUSUALLY LARGE STOMACH

The stomach is large, in big breeds nearly as big as that of a horse—ten times its bulk. The volume is very great compared with the intestine which succeeds it. As already indicated, this means that what the stomach digests best will be the suitable basic diet. And the physiologists show that protein, or more simply meat, is the complex organic material upon which the gastric juices are designed to act and to break up into simpler compounds that can later be absorbed in the intestinal tube and used by the body. In a healthy animal not too degenerated by human malpractice in breeding, the gastric juice contains sufficient hydrochloric acid to soften bone and release the soluble lime salts the body needs as well as the insoluble lime which helps to create that rather firm motion which is normal to the healthy dog.

When the stomach has broken down the lumps of food into a uniform broth-like fluid, it is ready to be passed on to the small intestine for further processing. The time taken for this to occur varies with the diet. Thus a high proportion of fat in the meal will slow up gastric digestion, as will large lumps of tough fibrous meat. This may often be an advantage. In any case, both puppies and dogs can be given large pieces of meat, without the need of preliminary mincing, without any harm and with the consequent steadying up of stomach digestion over a longer period. Also, the tearing up of large pieces gives the teeth and gums very necessary exercise, massaging the gums and checking the deposit of tartar, which is the bugbear of a starch diet, leading to premature loss of teeth in so many pets, not to mention dental operations at frequent intervals.

Dog biscuits are an excellent source of carbohydrate, and necessary under domestication when meat is so expensive. But I do draw the line at sales talk which recommends a biscuit *at bedtime*! This ensures a fermenting sludge of starch round the base of the teeth all night. No! The time for biscuit is prior to meat. It is the latter, best attached to a large bone, that will clean the teeth at bedtime and ensure dental longevity.

In the intestine, the outpouring of the digestive juices from the liver renders the contents alkaline. The pancreas and the glands lining the gut all produce a number of digestive ferments acting upon the fats and starches. As fast as each food constituent is broken down chemically to a certain molecular dimension, its absorption into the body ensues. The movement of the tube, too, churns up and mixes the contents and, together with its great length, ensures that every particle of energy-giving nourishment

Border Terrier

is absorbed, leaving only an indigestible residue to be voided as fæces.

It is important to remember that although the range of substances capable of digestion by the modern dog is wide, sudden changes, such as from biscuit to meat or *vice versa*, are productive of temporary indigestion. Once the digestive fluids have been habituated to certain food products, they cannot change their proportions of ferments at once, so that *diet changes should be adopted gradually over a period of days*.

It is impossible to lay down an ideal diet for all dogs. The diet sheet of a racing greyhound or working sheepdog must obviously contain more concentrated and greater quantities of energy-giving material than will that of an idle lapdog in a town. One can, however, give over-all guidance. Empirically, the quantity that keeps a dog still active, without on the one hand loss of weight and on the other progressive deposition of reserves of fat, is the correct one for it. While admitting that raw meat is the ideal form of protein to combine with carbohydrate for the dog, we must take into consideration the fact that there is a world-wide shortage of meat, and the prohibitive price is going to make it quite impractical to feed raw meat to pets. Young growing puppies fed solely on lean steak will develop rickets after being on this diet only four weeks. A balanced diet of protein and carbohydrate is essential. There are now available several different varieties of commercially produced ration for dogs and those produced by the brand leaders form excellent and easily fed diets, without the hazards to human health which are present if animal quality raw meat is fed. Some dog breeders still feel that there is virtue in going to the slaughter house and collecting carcase meat for their animals. In fact, such meat should be handled with the utmost caution, and knives and chopping boards sterilized after use. Tinned meats, made by well-known manufacturers, are extremely reliable. The balance of minerals is restored to compensate for those lost during cooking, and such meats present probably the cleanest, freshest and most trouble free method of feeding the dog. Unless the tin is marked "complete diet" they should be fed in the ratio 50:50 with a ground wholemeal biscuit meal, or brown bread. Such tinned meats contain all the additives in the way of necessary vitamins, so there is no need to give any tablets, powders or chocolate drops in addition. In fact, to do so can be actively harmful, as just as many bone dystrophies are caused by over vitaminization as lack of vitamins.

If raw meat is being fed, the formula is:

$\frac{1}{2}$ lb. of raw meat.
$\frac{1}{2}$ lb. biscuit meal or brown bread.
1 teaspoonful of sterilized bone flour.
1 drop of fresh cod-liver oil.

The vitamin content of cod-liver oil varies with the storage life of the product, so buy a little at a time. The quantity of $\frac{1}{2}$ lb. meat can be reduced or increased according to breed needs, but the meal, bone flour and cod-liver oil must be kept in proportion. The best biscuit meal is a plain wholemeal one, that make no pretensions to have vitamins or meat added. The smallest grade is best used throughout life for all breeds and sizes, to prevent the dreaded disease of bloat, or stomach distension. Meal should be fed soaked, in plain water or broth, with a few hard biscuits given early in the day. Bones with a little raw meat adhering are excellent as entertainment and teeth cleaners, and the gnawing action helps jaw development in puppies. The bone must be a very large marrow bone, and if there is more than one dog in the family, they should be given bones separately. More intense feelings are provoked by bones than any other dog possession.

The most modern method of feeding dogs is by the use of a complete feed based on vegetable protein. These foods look similar to biscuit meal but are a complete diet and the dog needs only fresh water in addition. Water must be constantly available, as this type of food has the natural water content extracted. In big kennels this type of food is hopper-fed, dry, and the dogs have access to eat as much as they wish. Many generations have lived on this food, and bred well, and have never tasted any thing else. The dog that is kept as a household pet is apt to get a little choosy, and to cater for this factor, it is possible to add up to 25 per cent of meat to the complete diet without spoiling the balance. The addition of this amount of eggs, meat or cheese does not increase the nutritional value, but it does increase acceptability and keeps up the dog's interest in food. Eggs, if given, must always be cooked, as raw egg white can produce a deficiency of the vitamin biotin, giving dermatitis, hair loss and poor growth. A small quantity of any of the tinned meats may be added, or the complete feeds may be soaked in chicken broth or vegetable water. Many

Boxer

puppies are now successfully weaned on to complete foods, and if they are kept on this regime, they do exceedingly well and the feeding is a minimal trouble to their owners. No vitamin supplement is necessary. Adult dogs are fed twice daily, a small meal in the morning and the larger one about 6 p.m. Puppies at nine weeks, when they go to their new homes, are on four meals a day, to coincide with human meal times. As the stomach capacity of the pup increases meals are dropped until the adult regime is reached at eighteen months, by which time maximum growth will have been achieved in all but the giant breeds.

Dog owners are always very puzzled about the amount

of food their dog needs. As with human beings, one dog will grow fat on the same quantity of food as will leave another lean. The dog that follows a farm tractor all day will need more food than the one that watches from a window. As a guide, it may be said that a young dog needs a diet based on half ounce of meat to each pound of bodyweight. An adult dog needs one third ounce meat to each pound of bodyweight, giving a spaniel weighing 30 lbs., some 10 ozs. raw meat, 10 ozs. biscuit meal, just over one teaspoonful of bone flour, and one drop of cod-liver oil daily. The same spaniel would require 1 lb. 4 oz. of complete diet canned food . . . e.g. "Chappie", or 10 ozs. of complete air dry diet, e.g. "Purina".

These quantities are for a dog on "maintenance" routine. More food is required for the growing dog, and the pregnant or lactating bitch.

FEEDING THE PREGNANT BITCH

The bitch needs no alteration in the amount of her diet until after the fourth week of pregnancy, when you should have a good indication of whether there are to be puppies or not. The bitch carries her young for nine weeks. During the first three weeks of gestation the bodies, limbs and tail develop, and for the final six weeks they grow. During the last five weeks of pregnancy the bitch's food, especially the protein content, should be increased to about 70 per cent more than maintenance level. If feeding raw meat, remember to increase the bone flour and cod-liver oil as well. She will need this to form the skeletons of her puppies. On the commercially produced rations the increase in volume taken will take care of all the vitamin supplementation necessary.

Meals should be given three or four times a day towards the end of pregnancy, as it will be found that the bitch cannot take a large amount of food at one time.

For all dogs, fresh water should be available always.

The traditional lump of sulphur in the bowl is harmless, and also useless and quite unnecessary.

Bitches Milk Supplement for Weaning and Orphan Puppies

Bitches milk is very different in analysis from cows milk. Goats milk is nearer, if it can be obtained. Use it at blood heat. If cow milk must be used, adapt it as follows:

Whisk together: 1 pint Channel Island milk, 1 oz. Casilan protein food and $\frac{1}{2}$ oz. edible corn oil.

Full cream milk powder is not suitable for puppies, and indeed many adult dogs cannot tolerate it, owing to the high lactose content, which causes diarrhoea.

Borzoi

CHAPTER IV

HOUSING, CLOTHES, TOILET AND EXERCISE

HOUSING

AFTER considering the habits of dogs, gaining insight into the art of acquiring them and learning the principles underlying their feeding, the next step is to house them appropriately.

Baskets are draughty, very tempting to chew and cannot be cleaned easily, so this traditional bed for the dog is supremely unsuitable. A puppy's first bed should be a cardboard carton, which can be changed as he chews it, or outgrows it. A rug or an old woolly will make his bedclothes. Plastic foam cushions are luxurious for the older dog who has learnt not to destroy. Later on a wooden box, which can be periodically scrubbed, can be bought or carpentered at home. For small- and medium-sized dogs, fibre glass beds can be bought, some of which incorporate a gentle heating panel in the base. If more than one dog is kept, they can sleep outside in a kennel, with an enclosed run for daytime. Civilized people have almost given up the habit of chaining a dog to an open kennel, and even the "running wire" method of restraint is seldom seen today. This kind of treatment makes a dog frustrated and savage. The good guard dog will guard his master's property fearlessly, because it is his home and territory. The sight of a dog free inside fenced property is the best deterrent against intruders. A chained dog sounds ferocious, but can be evaded.

A kennel may be built by a handyman, or there are many commercially built ones available. The kennel should be sited in a place sheltered from wind, and so that the dogs may sit in the doorway in the sun. Part of the kennel, or the run should be shaded from sunshine, as a small closed building can become intolerable in the summer.

The floor should be raised above the ground with care taken that rats do not live underneath. Walls should be lined and insulated, and an opening window, of wire reinforced glass provided. The ideal kennel has two compartments; one a small sleeping section with a raised bed, and the other for feeding, play, or excretion if the inmates are confined for long at a time. For outside bedding much the best plan is to purchase a bale of woodwool. It is very tightly packed, and will last a long time. Woodwool has a pleasant piney smell and will clean the dogs' coats. Straw and hay may well be damp, and will certainly harbour mites and insects, to cause skin irritation. There is also the danger that hay and straw stacks have been infested by rats, whose urine carries the dreaded disease, hepatitis. To use such straw is an expensive economy indeed. If you aim to keep a dog, then your garden must be fenced to above the height which he can jump . . . this may be seven feet for a boxer. Should your grounds be too extensive to fence all round, then a compound must be made where the dog can be safely put when you are busy elsewhere. Chain link fencing can be used, or welded wire panels.. The wire must be buried in the ground several inches, or the dogs will dig their way under it. You can save height on the fence by attaching an eighteen-inch wide strip at the top to project inwards at 45 degrees.

Many firms specialize in the manufacture of dog kennels, as well as beds and all other accessories, and their catalogues can be consulted.

CLOTHING

Provided a dog gets sufficient calories from his food, the only necessary clothes, summer and winter, are his collar and lead. While special coats are made and sold, many of them ornate and adorned with their owner's monogram, illness apart, they are best ignored. They make dogs delicate and the skin loses its gift of quick adaptation to changes of temperature. It is therefore best to regard clothing as unnecessary to a healthy individual, however short his coat of hair.

The collar serves as a means of attaching the lead, by which the dog is kept to hand in traffic, and also as a means of attaching a brass plate on which the owner's

Bulldog

name and address is engraved, for purposes of identification if the dog should go astray. This is a legal requirement and if not obeyed may lead to fines, particularly if the annual licence has not been taken out and the dog has been detained at a police station as a stray.

One occasionally sees dogs being led about with breast harness instead of a collar. This usually indicates that the early training of the dog, not to pull its owner along, has been omitted. There also exists in the minds of some people the idea that a collar throttles a dog and is in some measure, therefore, cruel. I should imagine the cumbersome straps of the harness far more troublesome to the dog, if his opinion could be asked.

Some collars are heavily studded with metal as a protection from bites in the vulnerable throat region. Here again the weight and size of such collars leads to discomfort, which *in toto* must far exceed the remote contingency it aims at preventing.

THE TOILET

Most dogs benefit by a few minutes' daily brushing. It brings up the lustre of the short, shiny coat and, combined with the comb, is a necessity for the long-coated breeds. With these latter, matted hair requires frequent combing out, and mud must be removed in wet weather. A good tip for long-haired dogs that return wet and muddy from a walk is to dust them liberally with bran or sawdust and to brush this out before the dog enters the house. This constitutes a form of "dry-cleaning" which is as good as a bath.

Many breeds have their coats shortened, either all over, as in the case of terriers, or locally—often in weird designs—as with poodles. This process of stripping certainly saves the housekeeper much sweeping up of shed hair, and most people think it improves the appearance of the animal. It is claimed that it helps the animal to endure hot weather, though it is open to question whether an unstripped dog feels the heat more than his stripped fellow. After all, in hot climates the Arab dons a blanket to keep off the sun and its excessive ultra-violet rays, so there is something to be said against stripping where sunlight is intense and prolonged.

Stripping is, however, an established custom, both with pets and for the show ring. For the latter, a skilled stripper, by leaving a little more hair here and taking off a little more there, can to quite an extent enhance the physical perfections of his exhibit to the current fashion in contours—an advantage not possessed by human contestants at beauty shows!

Baths of the ordinary soap-and-water type are an occasional necessity. Whether from mud and dirt, or following upon an ancestral urge to roll upon some putrefied carcass found in the course of a walk, a thorough wash all over is sometimes required, and with ordinary care is harmless and can be repeated as often as may be socially necessary. Dog hair is constituted differently from human hair, and a special dog shampoo should be used on the dog. Pet shops will have a wide selection, some

Cairn Terrier

with insecticidal content, others tinted to suit various shades of coat. Water should be only lukewarm, and the shampoo thoroughly rinsed out with a spray attachment. Towel dry, then take for a short run on the lead. If you let him loose he will throw himself down and roll in the nearest pile of dirt available. Really big dogs which will not fit into the kitchen sink have to wait for a hot day and are bathed in the garden. Have one bucket of shampoo water and several others for rinsing. Better put your swimsuit on before you start, as you will get as wet as the dog. The big dog who has got himself objectionably dirty in cold weather must be sponged clean bit by bit and not totally immersed.

Detergents in the form of washing up liquids or washing

powder should not be used on a dog's coat, except in small patches to remove tar or grease. Although one can sympathize with the housewife who does not want dirt brought into the house, it is not a good practice to wash a dog's feet in antiseptic or detergent after every outing. Crumpled newspaper does a good job in removing the worst mud and the final cleaning can be done with an old towel. For the long-coated dog, dry cleaning powders are available which are shaken into the coat and brushed out, taking grease and dirt with them. There is also a foam, presented in an aerosol can, which cleans up specially dirty areas, and is extensively used on show dogs just before they enter the judging ring. Your pet shop will have all these aids to doggy beauty, and more.

Exercise

In towns, most dogs have to be taken out for a few miles' walk each day. In the country, many of the smaller breeds get all that is necessary in their constant exploration of the garden. It is well to bear in mind that a dog can cover at least twice as much ground as his two-legged companion running free in the course of a walk. The need for road discipline will be dealt with elsewhere, but in these days of cars, it is best to have an invariable rule to keep the dog on the lead until the open space or park is reached, if accidents are to be avoided.

The need for water to drink on return from exercise must always be remembered, particularly in hot weather. A pinch of salt (a level teaspoon to a pint of water) in the drinking-water supplies the salt lost by evaporation from the mouth and tongue (which largely replaces skin perspiration in the dog), for in getting rid of the excess therms generated by exercise, quite an appreciable quantity of salt leaves the body in this manner and must be replaced by some means or other.

CHAPTER V

TRAINING

CONFIDENCE BETWEEN MASTER AND DOG

A PUPPY coming as a raw recruit to a new home and master, requires considerable patience and understanding. Left to himself, he will develop under the influence of his subconscious instincts, many of which are undesirable under domestic conditions. Some of these instincts have to be suppressed, others can be made use of and guided into special channels.

The master and teacher attains something like the status of deity in the doggy mind, and that implies considerable responsibility towards the pupil. There used to be two schools of thought in the mode or attitude to be adopted. One, based upon the Biblical exhortation, "The fear of the Lord is the beginning of wisdom", regarded a good hiding as the best overture to the relationship. I have met gamekeepers within recent years who still maintain that this is the quickest way to get through the training of a gun-dog. It may be true for certain limited actions that have to be inculcated, but is best forgotten, the results obtained from the alternative method being infinitely superior.

This second method is dependent upon the creation of the deepest possible affection and trust between master and pupil from the outset. Infinite patience and an ability to view each situation as it arises with doggy eyes are the keys to success. To build up this affection and trust, the whole routine of the puppy's life must be undertaken by the teacher. Most important of all is that of food, for the way to the heart is via the stomach.

It is also a notable fact among most species of animals,

that, if adopted early by a foster-parent, and we can include the love and care of men and women in this category, the orphan tends to develop a fixation for life towards this one foster parent. None other will command such undivided attention and affection.

Once this mutual confidence is established, the simplest lessons can be begun. They consist of inculcating the habit of asking to go out of doors to make water and defecate. Knowledge of natural habits shows that puppies almost always pass water after waking, and pass water and fæces soon after feeding. So be on the watch at these times. Imitate the tongue of the bitch, which licks round the excretory orifices to stimulate excretion, with gentle tickling by the finger. This will trigger off the act. This is known as "pottying". Mistakes, when they do happen, must be met with signs of displeasure, or if need be a smack, and always removal out of doors. Association of ideas, one of the sheet anchors of the teacher, comes in here and soon the urge to urinate becomes associated, by trial and error, with going through a door into the garden, and the successful performance of the ritual brings praise from master and joy to the pupil that he is the cause of pleasure to his god.

Repetition daily of whatever lesson is being undertaken is another obvious necessity. But commonly these lessons are too long, and attention wanders with weariness of spirit. Two sessions of five minutes, with a few hours between, may give quicker results than one session of ten minutes. The more the lesson can be presented in the form of a game, the better.

PUNISHMENT

Punishment for naughtiness, inattentiveness, deliberate "try-ons" and disobedience must of course be visited with chastisement. But the punishment *must* fit the crime. To a sensitive puppy a look of horror or a word uttered in a disapproving tone is often enough. To another, nothing short of a sharp cut with a whip and signs of master's extreme displeasure will achieve any result. The fatal thing is loss of temper. The whole process of schooling can be ruined by injudicious punishment. Also, the animal must be caught *in flagrante delicto*. To come into a room half an hour after a puddle has been made on the carpet and to proceed to whip a puppy just doesn't make

Chow Chow

sense to the poor victim and has no association in his mind with the crime.

One of the most valuable associative weapons is the use of a chosen word as the trigger to initiate the sequence of nerve reactions that have been learned. The word is best monosyllabic and should be easily distinguished from all others used in training. Words like "heel", "down", "sit", and "drop" are familiar and have been used for generations. The use of a whistle is common and the pattern can be varied for each duty it accompanies; and it has the advantage of carrying over long distances. It is worth noting that the ear of the dog is capable of accepting sound waves higher than those received by the human ear; and a whistle has been used for dogs (especially in war-time) which is inaudible to human ears.

Dogs will also respond to hand and arm signals, which are used both with gun and sheepdogs.

The art of retrieving is generally started early at home with a bundled-up rabbit skin. This is thrown for the dog to bring back and drop at the feet of his master. Starting as a great game, it becomes a habit long before the puppy goes out with a gun and is expected to bring in rabbits and birds.

The use of an adult trained animal is also of great assistance in the more advanced lessons. Sheepdogs are frequently "finished" by this means and learn by observation of their elders.

The reader is referred to the text-books on training mentioned in the bibliography for more precise details of training, based upon these principles.

FAULTS AND VICES

As with the human race, there are born crooks, morons and incurable idlers among dogs. Only long experience will show the teacher whether it is worth persevering to eradicate these faults. Generally speaking, a fault that is not tackled during puppyhood, and which has been allowed to persist after the first year of life, is hard, if not impossible, to cure. Viciousness, particularly to human beings and in the larger breeds, must be regarded as a potential source of danger in the future. Persistent stealing of food, despite correction, is a vice that is hardly worth tolerating in a house pet.

The pursuit of cats, chickens, and the worrying of flocks of sheep, can be expensive indulgences. Actually a primal normal instinct, it wants to be rigorously guarded against and checked from the outset. The presence of a cat in the household usually renders a puppy unlikely to regard cats as prey. Familiarity with chickens, which can be obtained by kennelling a puppy in a chicken run on a chain for short periods, goes a long way to driving home the subconscious realization that chickens are part of master's entourage and therefore sacrosanct.

Pulling on the lead is all too common even in dogs of mature age, and can be easily checked in most instances if firmly taken in hand during puppyhood. Gently jerk the animal back whenever he starts to pull, insisting gently but firmly that the lead must slacken before you proceed. Accompany each jerk with a suitable monosyllable such as "back" and it soon becomes a settled habit.

A lot of nonsense is talked about the "choke" collar, in which one end passes through the other, to be attached to the lead. When a boisterous young dog tries to pull his owner, and successfully, after him during walks, this collar is the sole means by compression of the windpipe, of checking this dangerous and undignified procession. Of course, in rough hands it is a potential source of suffering, but it should not be banned or altogether condemned on these grounds, since it teaches the lesson not to pull on the lead in minutes where guile, entreaties, threats and hidings take hours, and moreover may fail. And after one or two walks with the choke collar, the lesson learned, the normal collar is resumed, and for the future a gentle tug is all that the pupil needs to make him decelerate, and stop pulling your arms out of their sockets.

Sheep Worrying

Once a dog has gained a taste for pursuing sheep, the problem is very difficult, and one escapade may involve his owner in a claim for damages totalling a hundred pounds or more. An old shepherd once told me his recipe for the cure. It was to put a dog collar on a vigorous ram, attach it with about two feet of chain to the collar of the dog, and set the two animals loose in a good-sized field. The ram then led the dog a merry gallop until he became sated with sheep and, when released, had imprinted upon his mind such a memory that he would never again approach a flock with anything other than trepidation! It seems to me to be a rational procedure, but difficult to organize when required in suburban areas. Other than this method, I know of no cure, though the birth of the instinct to pursue can be kept buried by familiarity with sheep during walks, and by checking the signs of desire

Corgi

for pursuit. Tying a dead chicken to a poultry chaser is said likewise by country folk to engender a life-long distaste for further pursuit of the domestic fowl.

It is a fact that established pets quickly learn what is master's and what is alien property. Thus a perfect sheep dog has been known to kill and eat the lambs of a neighbour, though blameless at home. "Foreign" cats and next door chickens will be pursued though at home the offender will sleep with the home cat and be safe in the home fowl run.

Ferocity to other dogs may be due to more than one cause. In some, it is the bullying characteristic of a gross, domineering nature. In others, it is the reaction of an inferiority complex to potential danger, with an instinct to get the offensive going before the other fellow suspects trouble—*bis dat qui cito dat*. Many of our modern neurotic, over-bred dogs are aggressive from this cause; and the over-loving indulgence of a large number of women to their pets—with failure to deal with snappiness to strangers and visitors "because it would be cruel to hit the poor darling"—often spoils the character of a dog, rendering him as selfish and unkind as any child would be under a similar regime. Pampering is often more omission than commission, and certainly as harmful.

HANDLING A DOG FIGHT

When a fight occurs, the reaction of owners is often flustered and futile for want of a cool head and quick thinking. To dive into the mêlée without any plan leads, as often as not, to injury to the human and is as foolish as standing by helplessly or wasting time in upbraiding the other owner. Sudden shocks will often temporarily arrest the battle and will provide an opportunity for separating the contestants. A bucket of cold water, thrown over both animals, a lighted newspaper waved close to the heads of the fighters, an attack of sneezing engendered by the pepper castor, are all proved arresters. But the ensuing dive for the contestants by the respective owners must not be delayed or the battle may be renewed. It is not advisable to pull two dogs apart by the collars unless the hands are gloved, for the bites inflicted while a dog is "berserk" with rage are not as a rule minor affairs. A fight is very difficult to stop if you are singlehanded; possibly the best way is to create a diversion. It may be possible to twist the collar of the aggressor and cut off the air supply temporarily, at which stage they must be separated quickly.

During the two occasions—in spring and autumn— when bitches are commonly on heat, fighting is inevitable among the males that congregate as near the home of the desired female as they dare. Most owners of bitches have them boarded away during these occasions. While the essential oils (which, by their masking odour, are used to prevent dogs following a bitch), have a camouflage value, it should be mentioned that these precautions are quite useless once a dog has discovered the home of a bitch on heat. He will keep his three weeks' vigil with the rest of the parish dogs once the news has gone abroad!

Recently it has been found that one of the products of chlorophyll, after a process of irradiation during manufacture, provides a means of deodorizing the bitch on heat

Dachshund

so effectively that although herself ready for intercourse, the dog, whose release of erotic behaviour seems to be entirely "triggered" by the heat odour, is not excited at all. The results of giving this product—sold as Amplex—in tablets, and as a lotion for washing over the hind-quarters is that, provided the frequency of dosage is correct, the bitch may be taken for walks, and the congregation of followers and hangers-on round the home entirely ceases.

Veterinary surgeons are often consulted about sex perversions in dogs. The dog that "rides" the legs of humans can be quickly cured of the habit if his prostate gland is evacuated. The male dog that seems attractive to other dogs, and is always being an embarrassment to his owner in public places, is usually afflicted with an infection of the anal glands that gives the secretion an odour suggestive of the female on heat. This again is amenable to treatment. Yet many dogs with one or other of these habits are taken to be destroyed through ignorance or prudery on the part of their owners, when in fact the cure is quite simple.

Dandie Dinmont

CHAPTER VI

BREEDING

At the beginning of 1945, I was permitted to refer to dogs in a broadcast talk for the first time since I began working for the B.B.C. The talk I gave created a good deal of interest, was reproduced in the *Listener*, and printed in leaflet form by one of the animal protection societies.

One of my points was that the breeding of dogs was far too haphazard an affair and not sufficiently based on available knowledge. In addition, I pointed out some of the reprehensible things that were going on and cited the crossing of the Borzoi into our Collie in order to secure a long narrow head in place of one of the broadest and brainiest of doggy skulls, with disastrous results on the temperament and intelligence. I gave other instances equally foolish, but the aim of what I said was a plea that all this unfortunate hit and miss experimental breeding could be put on a much surer and scientific basis if representatives of my profession, geneticists, and the Kennel Club, could meet and discuss the problem.

In the thirty years which have passed since that time there has been a tremendous advance in dog breeding. More veterinary surgeons are specializing in small animal practice, and the British Small Animal Veterinary Association regularly puts on lectures for breeders, so that knowledge and experience may be exchanged. Breeders are becoming more and more aware of the disasters caused by indiscriminate breeding. The Kennel Club and the British Veterinary Association have together organized an examination system to detect Hip Dysplasia and several eye diseases. All dogs offered for public stud in the affected breeds should be submitted for examination.

A recent book on genetics as applied to dog-breeding will be found mentioned under Books to Read (p. 117) and is recommended. First worked out by plant genetecists, and applied with enormous success in horticulture and agricultural crops, it has extended to the farm animals, cattle in particular. The would-be dog breeder should study as well such a work as Hagedoorn's *Animal Breeding* (which has a chapter devoted to dogs) before commencing work.

QUESTIONABLE FOLK-LORE

The old belief that a bitch that has had a litter of mongrels is no longer of use to mate to a pedigree dog still continues, although proved to the hilt to be untrue. That the size of one or other parent determines the ease or difficulty of the ensuing birth is another fallacy. There is no necessity for any bitch to have a litter. The legend still persists that it is essential for her to have one lot of puppies, but this is quite untrue, and unless you have some special reason and interest in breeding, it is better to leave it alone. As with the human population, reproduction can bring about uterine troubles just as often as does the non-use of those organs. Some maiden bitches suffer from phantom pregnancies in which they mimic the entire process of pregnancy, down to making a bed and producing milk. To have an actual litter is no cure, rather does it intensify the desire for more puppies. The only answer is to have the bitch spayed.

BREEDING

Never consider having a litter from a bitch purely to make some money. Dog breeding is a very hazardous occupation, and you could easily lose money, or at best, break even. You should have a considerable amount of capital available before you begin, as you have a lot of money to expend on mating, advertising, and feeding bitch and puppies before you see any return. When you have decided to mate your bitch, you should seek out a stud dog long before she comes into season. You would be well advised to go to an established breeder, possibly the kennels where you first bought the puppy, for professional advice and help. The breeder will know about bloodlines, and the diseases prevalent in the breed. She will be able to

Elkhound

assess the faults in your bitch and recommend a dog who can compensate for them. If you use a pet dog, belonging to a friend, on your bitch, you are giving yourself a handi- cap from the start. Not only will the dog not be accom- plished at stud work (and it does not always come naturally) but no-one will know what quality and type of stock he will throw. The pet dog will probably not have been screened for hereditary diseases, some of which are impossible to detect without professional examination, and most important of all, you will lose all the marketing advantages that the experienced breeder can bring you. Famous stud dogs have waiting lists for their puppies, and these customers might be sent on to you, if you rear the litter well. The stud fee of a professional dog, which may range from £12 to £50 according to breed, is well worth the money paid for it. The Kennel Club can direct you to a stud dog in your area, or you will find them advertised in the dog weeklies.

It is usual to mate a bitch between the 10th and 14th day of her heat, when the vulva should be most swollen, and the red discharge has just stopped. The stud dog must be booked on the very first day the bitch "shows colour". If you are having a bitch mated, it is wise to test the vulva every day with a white tissue, when the heat is imminent, to be sure you know exactly when she starts.

It should be understood that it is necessary for the dog to become locked to the bitch during mating, so that he cannot get free from her for approximately twenty minutes. Without this "tie", fertilization is doubtful.

PREGNANCY AND AFTER

The only special attention the bitch needs during the sixty-three days of pregnancy is an increase of food. She may be expected to require twice the usual quantity after the puppies arrive. During the last fortnight, she will naturally be less active but should receive exercise within her powers every day. The whelping kennel should be capable of being darkened; and if some means of spying on the bitch during the event, without entering to disturb her pains, can be devised, this is a great help. It is also important that the bitch should become accustomed to the kennel some days before the birth. It is a great mistake to carry off a bitch to strange quarters at the commencement of labour. This custom, together with the insistence of owners of sitting with the bitch continually while labour is in progress, have a good deal to do with the hold-up of labour pains. In silence, near-darkness, and freedom from distraction, one approaches the conditions that obtain under natural circumstances.

There will, of course, be occasions when, for one reason or another, there is a hold-up in the arrival of the puppies. If it is found that one of the puppies (usually a large one in a tiny litter, the product of a forced union!) has descended from the pelvis of the bitch, is just visible externally but will not move any further, despite good pains, then one can grasp whatever is available and pull gently in tempo with the labour pains. A slight rotation of the pup, first one way, then the other, often resolves

English Collie

the hitch when it is due to a limb. In the case of a puppy arriving tail first, the friction of the hair can be very considerable and may cause difficulty; also, in this presentation, at the exhausting climax of expulsion, the head reaches the bony arch of the pelvis and may be the cause of the hold-up.

The beginner should not attempt internal examinations but should get expert help if such intervention appears necessary. Do not be alarmed if several hours elapse between the onset of pains and the first arrival; this is common with a first litter. Nor is it unusual for the bitch to take a long rest between two births. So long as her condition is good, this period of recuperation is normal in many instances. If, however, the natural methods of mating have been followed, these large puppies of the small litter will not occur, and the attentions of the obstetrician will not be necessary, for the puppies will be numerous and therefore each one will be small enough at birth to arrive easily and speedily.

During a slow birthing, particularly in cold weather, it may be wise to take each puppy from the bitch as it arrives, and wrap it in a blanket over a warm bottle. The puppies can be restored to their dam as soon as she has finished her labour.

With a bitch having a first family, the initial flow of milk may be satisfactory; but each teat is best tested to make sure that the milk emerges when gently stripped between finger and thumb. Complete absence of milk is of course a serious matter, and is difficult to remedy. Professional advice should be sought at once if this is the state of affairs. Whilst as a rule a puppy finds its own way to its teat, there may be a weakling requiring guidance to the source of nourishment as well as protection from a tyrant brother or sister who may drive him away from the breast. Such protection may take the form of taking away the strong feeders after they have suckled for a few moments, and leaving the weakling to take his fill alone, before restoring the others to the breast.

Do not let a bitch whelp in straw or on anything other than a cloth or towel. Hay or straw is apt to get entangled in the umbilical cord and afterbirth, and may make it impossible for the mother to sever the cord. This she does instinctively with her teeth, prior to washing her new babe all over. She very rarely requires human aid in this ritual, unless she has been fussed over throughout the event.

It is also important not to let admiring humans near the family for at least a day. Instinctively, the bitch is wildly apprehensive, and may even devour her babes rather than let them fall into the hands of the stranger. Wait until this instinct is replaced by maternal pride and she almost asks you to come and admire her children, as she will within two or three days.

Sometimes it is judged that the number of puppies is too much for the bitch to nurse. Unless they are of great potential value, it is the easiest course to eliminate the necessary number, weaklings usually being the first to go. Foster mothers can be obtained but it is a difficult procedure to carry out and only advisable with valuable pedigree stock. Bringing up on the bottle by hand is a superhuman task, involving night and day feeding, and is almost beyond the endurance of one individual single handed. Moreover, it is often unsuccessful and the puppies are very likely to fade out after a few days for no ascertainable reason.

FEEDING THE PUPPIES

Weaning is an automatic process conditioned by the arrival of the puppies' teeth. These prove so painful to the bitch during suckling that round about the fifth week she will be getting impatient of her children, allowing only short feeds; then it is time to provide food for the puppies. Milk is the basis of the first diet but if cows' milk is used, it must be modified (see page 47) as to the proportion of its constituents if it is not to set up indigestion. In country districts, goat milk can often be obtained and is excellent for feeding purposes. Tinned milk-substitutes are available.

It is not wise to dispose of the puppies until they are capable of feeding themselves and are entirely independent of their dam. Usually, after eight weeks, they can go to new homes. This is always an ordeal, and it is most important that the food at the new home should as far as possible be identical in nature and quantity, and should be given at the same hours as previously. So many puppies develop bowel trouble through neglect of this precaution.

There is a practice among owners of stud dogs to offer the services of a sire in exchange for the first choice of a puppy from the litter. This is often an unhappy arrangement for the owner of the bitch. If the family consists of only two or three, it may mean that all that is left is one or more relatively unsaleable pet puppies, the one potential champion having been taken. It is much better to

Golden Retriever

pay the stud fee and keep the disposal of the whole of the litter in your own hands. If the mating proves fruitless, it is understood as a rule that a second mating will be given free or at a reduced charge; but it is as well to have a clear understanding on this point at the time of the first mating.

DEALING WITH THE PROMISCUOUS BITCH

If a bitch goes astray, there is no need for her to have a litter in consequence. Stilboestrol, injected within 24 hours, will prevent fertilization occurring, but may affect her future breeding potential. It is better to have the litter and reduce the number of puppies to two soon after birth.

It is often difficult to diagnose the existence of pregnancy in the bitch. Sometimes an X-ray photograph will clinch the matter, but owing to the very late deposition of lime salts in the skeletons of the fœtuses, a negative X-ray photograph is not a certain proof that the bitch is non-pregnant. Unfortunately, too, virgin bitches with strong leanings towards maternity develop what is known as false or ghost pregnancy. During the weeks following a heat, apart from any question of mating, they will develop a secretion of milk in the glands and the abdomen will enlarge, giving a general picture that pregnancy exists. This is a well-known booby trap to the veterinary surgeon but can be terminated rapidly by modern drug treatment.

Griffon Bruxellois

CHAPTER VII

DOG SHOWS

WITHOUT the Dog Show, the dog would never have reached the status he holds to-day. The Show is the shop window of the breeder and fancier. Without the endorsement of judges and Kennel Club certificates gained in open competition, the high values of British breeds of dog would never have been reached.

The lowest ranking show is the Kennel Club Exemption Show, at which entries can be made on the day. Dogs participating need not be registered with the Kennel Club, and indeed there are usually some novelty classes for the longest wagging tail, or the most beautiful eyes, in which crossbreds can be entered. Although informality is the keynote, it can be very difficult to win a prize at such a show, owing to the variety of breeds in each class. It is often easier for the beginner to make a start at a small Open Show, with classes for specific breeds, where like is judged against like. Entries for all shows except the Exemption Show are made several weeks in advance, to enable catalogues to be printed. The shows are advertised in the two dog newspapers, *Dog World* and *Our Dogs*.

A dog should never be taken to a show before it has been fully inoculated, or indeed for the two weeks following such inoculation. Now there is no general veterinary examination at shows, it is all the more important to avoid taking a sick dog there, and with the modern method of immunization there is no excuse for running into danger. Yet multitudes of people who know better, still take a chance on this, as do many who, knowing their exhibit is unwell, persist in taking him along and showing him, and as often as not acting as a centre of dissemination of disease. For, however fit and tough a dog may be, the excitement, the atmosphere, the handling by strangers, the crowding together, create an ideal medium for germs to take hold.

In this country, the Kennel Club is the absolute monarch of the Show Ring. It licenses the Shows and its rules have to be obeyed. Under normal conditions, there are some fifty Shows of championship status held each year, in addition to about two hundred others. A first prize under

Irish Wolfhound

Kennel Club rules must not be less than £2, a second half this sum, and a third half of the second in value. The Kennel Club was formed in 1873 and its functions comprise the registration of animals and their pedigrees, and the awarding of championships to the various breeds admitted to compete for this blue riband of the dog world. To become a full champion, a dog or bitch has to win a challenge certificate at three Shows under three different judges.

The novice would do well to attend a few Shows and get to know the ropes before attempting to compete. He needs to watch the judges at work, as well as the competitors, whose technique is nowadays extensive, not to say peculiar in many instances, in their endeavours to show off their pets to the best advantage. And, as judges are only human, with predilections for certain points, not always shared with equal vehemence by other judges, the frequenter of Shows soon learns the value of pursuing the judge around, whose views on canine perfection most coincide with the make-up of the novice dog it is designed shall appear before him.

The handling of an animal prior to its first Show and its preparation have become more and more the task of the specialist professional. Many amateur owners, of course, do this work themselves and do it quite successfully; but it has to be learned. The beginner needs to make friends with experts in these matters and watch them at work, preferably on animals of the breed he intends to exhibit himself. By doing this and by studying the books devoted to canine beauty culture, handling and showing, and by observation of the finished specimens at the actual Shows, he will come to gain the necessary skill. There is not a great deal of apparatus necessary. The stripping comb, scissors and a chalk block are all that many experts use to get the hairy coat into Show order. And by leaving a little more hair in the concave places and shaving closer on the convexities, it is astonishing what a lot of harmless but fruitful deception can be practised, so far as the judge's eye is concerned!

Most districts have their local canine society. By joining this and the society devoted to the particular breed in question, and by reading the columns of the doggy Press, knowledge that is essential to success should be picked up quite rapidly. And as you increase in stature and are on the road to being regarded as an authority, your turn may come to be a judge some day. It is a great responsibility. An unsound criterion by one individual of points necessary to make a dog a winner can influence a breed for the worse for generations, and slowly eliminate it from the scene by the demand made on stamina if the faulty criterion is persisted in. Is it too much to ask that the standards of Show points should be revised, with the well-being of the breed in mind? And may the committee that does this beneficient task have among its members an experienced veterinary surgeon accompanied by a genetecist? It is not fair to the dogs that they should not have

Kerry Blue Terrier

the benefit of what science can offer in this respect, and should be at the mercy of the partially enlightened or the ignorant theorist.

AFTER THE SHOW

For some days after bringing an exhibit back from a show, it should be carefully watched. If anything is noted amiss, such as loss of appetite, moping, the development of a temperature, undue itchiness of the skin, professional advice should be sought and the patient isolated meanwhile. It is in fact a wise precaution always to isolate under these conditions for at least a week, if the introduction of infection into a kennel is to be avoided sooner or later.

As nervousness of noise and crowds at the Show often results in the dog failing to look his best, it is important to get him used to noise and crowds at the earliest opportunity. Visits to busy shopping centres and railway stations should achieve this end. Try also to get him used to being mouthed and handled by strangers so that when you show him he will not resent this interference. The judge—and the Show veterinary surgeon too!—will be grateful to you for this mercy; and the former may award just that extra mark for good manners that may help you to head the list of competitors.

TRAVEL

All too often puppies are sent off by rail in dark boxes, unaccompanied, and as a result a nerve-racked exhausted creature arrives, often wet through lying on a urine soiled bed, and incubating a chill or worse. Dogs under a year should not be sent on long journeys unaccompanied. With older dogs, guards may require a muzzle to be put on —a trying experience until a dog has got used to wearing one. In cars many dogs are travel-sick. They travel best on the floor of the vehicle, where the apparent movements of hedges and horizon are not visible to disturb the eyes and lead to nausea. Your vet can supply a tranquillizing drug which will help to form a habit of travelling in the car without excitement. Air travel should be entrusted to one of the firms undertaking such transport who know the types of crate that are suitable. In any case domed-headed breeds such as Boxers, Bull-dogs and Pekes, should not be sent unaccompanied by air as they are liable to burst blood vessels when left alone in freight compartments, particularly in tropical heat.

Doping with sedatives and narcotics is not to be recommended, as the length of action is uncertain, and the lot of the half-dazed dog, coming round too soon, alone in a freight compartment is worse than if he had had no sedative at all.

Old English Sheep Dog

CHAPTER VIII

THE DOG AND THE LAW

No one who keeps a dog can avoid some degree of contact with the laws that have been enacted with the dog as their *raison d'être*. This chapter gives a summary of what an owner needs to know of his responsibilities and liabilities in this respect.

DOG LICENCES

The law of the land states that each dog must have a licence, with certain exemptions granted to masters of hounds, in respect of their packs, to farmers for a sheep or cattle dog, and to blind persons. Licences are obtainable at the Post Office. As the revenue from dog licences goes towards local rates, it is reasonable to buy one within the Borough in which you reside. It is a penal offence to keep a dog without a licence, which must be produced on request of an authorized person, such as a police officer.

IDENTIFICATION

Every dog using the highway must wear a collar or harness, on which can be plainly read his owner's name and address. An owner is expected to have control over his dog, and it is not permitted to be a nuisance or menace to others; though, no doubt, in the latter case the onus of proof is on the accuser. Many local authorities have their own bye-laws in relation to dogs, which can be read at a local police station. Occasionally, if a case of rabies occurs in the district, it may be necessary to muzzle all dogs when they are out of their homes.

STRAYS

When a police officer believes that any dog met on the highway or in a public place is a stray, he is empowered to seize and detain it until the owner has claimed it and paid the expenses incurred. If the animal has the owner's name and address on its collar, a notice will be sent by the police to the effect that the animal is detained and, if not claimed within seven clear days after the service of the notice, is liable to be disposed of or destroyed.

Anyone who picks up a stray must either return it to its owner or take it to the nearest police station, and must inform the police where it was found. They will then keep the dog as a stray. If the finder wishes to adopt the animal, he will, on fulfilling certain conditions laid down on a form provided for the purpose, be able to have it after seven days, if the owner has not claimed it within the specified period. Failure to comply with the regulations in these matters can lead to a fine.

DANGEROUS DOGS

If a complaint is made that a dog is dangerous and is not kept under proper control, any court of summary jurisdiction is empowered to make an order for it to be kept under adequate control or to order its destruction. The penalty for disobeying such an order can be a heavy fine for every day of default.

A dog which, in the opinion of the Justices, is mad may be treated in like manner and they have power to require all the dogs in the neighbourhood to be controlled. Of course, if the madness is due to infection by the rabies virus, the Ministry of Agriculture would step in and enforce the law as regards muzzling over the necessary area. Rabies is fortunately extinct in Great Britain now and is only liable to occur where dogs, which have become infected unknown to their owners, are brought into this country. Cases arise from time to time in kennels where dogs undergo their quarantine detention on arrival from abroad, and it also occurs and is a menace where dogs have been smuggled into the country to evade the quarantine regulations.

INJURIES

The owner of a dog is liable for any damage done to cattle (in law, "cattle" comprises horses, mules, asses, sheep, goats and swine) and poultry. It is not necessary to show previous propensity to such mischief or to prove neglect on the part of the owner of the dog.

To steal a dog is an offence punishable by imprisonment or fine. Killing or wounding leads to similar penalties. It is an offence to lay poison other than for vermin, and such poison must be suitably protected from domestic animals. Another offence under the Protection of Animals Act of 1911 is "carrying an animal in any manner or position so as to cause suffering". Prosecutions have been brought under this act against owners who left dogs shut in cars during hot weather. The Protection of Animals (Anaesthetics) Act of 1954 provides that anaesthetics must be administered for all but the most minor operations. Tail docking and removal of dew claws are excepted, provided they are done before the puppy's eyes are open. The Animals Act of 1971 altered the position at common law with regard to accidents caused by livestock. If your dog runs into the road, causing a cyclist to swerve, or gets its lead entangled in an old lady's walking stick, thereby doing her some injury, the question is simply one of negligence. The court will want to know whether you have taken all reasonable precautions to control your dog and prevent him getting loose. It is wise for every owner to have their pet covered for third party liability. Many Canine Societies and Organizations provide block cover for their members by a small addition to the annual subscription.

On the Road

The dog has the same right to the road as the pedestrian but he is also liable for the same sins as his master: loitering, crossing at the wrong place or time, or causing an obstruction. If a vehicle or person is injured as a result, the dog owner is liable in law and will have to pay up for him. On the other hand, the owner has his remedy if he suffers injury to his dog when the latter is using his road rights properly.

If a dog is run over, it is the duty of the motorist to stop, give his name and address to the owner, and, in the absence of a witness, the event must be reported to the nearest police station within twenty-four hours. If the motorist drives on—and many do—try to get his car number. If proved to be at fault, he will be liable for veterinary fees in case of injury that is not fatal.

In the absence of the owner, the police have power to act and may call in a veterinary surgeon, whose certificate is final and cannot be the subject of any claim for damages for wrongful destruction.

In the Fields

Gamekeepers, shepherds and farmers may only shoot a marauding dog among their flocks and herds if it actually saves the life of the pursued animal. Moreover, if the dog is maimed, they will be liable for damages and fees incurred in treatment. Prosecution for cruelty is also possible. A dog cannot be shot for trespassing only and notices to such an effect are not enforceable.

Damages—and very heavy ones at times—can be claimed in respect of injuries caused to sheep, game, poultry, etc., by a dog. If you are unfortunate enough to get a claim against you and cannot clearly prove an alibi, put the matter into the hands of a solicitor and make no admission of guilt or responsibility; and do not offer to settle privately.

It occasionally happens that a dog gets caught in a snare or trap when roaming over the countryside. The Pests Act of 1954 clearly states that "if for the purpose of killing hares or rabbits any person uses or knowingly permits the use of a spring trap, *elsewhere than in a rabbit hole*, he shall be liable to a fine". No traps must be set in the open.

BOARDING KENNELS

Boarding Kennels are licensed by the local authority, who each have their special requirements on the suitability of the premises for the accommodation of dogs. Kennels are licensed to board a specific number of dogs, and a register must be kept of the dogs in residence. Adequate fire precautions are essential.

SALE OF DOGS

The purchase of a dog involves purchaser and seller in certain mutual obligations. The former expects a healthy normal animal and also expects to get a square deal. Unfortunately, far too often the animal proves to have some defect or disease which is only recognized after leaving the seller's premises; and on the owner's return, the seller fails to give any satisfaction, usually on the grounds that what happens after the animal has left is no concern of his. Hints on how to handle this all-too-common situation have already been given in Chapter II. Mention, too, has been made of the obligation on the purchaser of making any complaint to the seller at once, if he is to be fair about the matter. Here again, if the differences appear irreconcilable, the less said at the time the better. Get a good solicitor to handle the affair for you.

The Trade Descriptions Act of 1968 applies to the sale of dogs. It is a criminal offence to apply a false description, be it for fitness of purpose, e.g. suitability as a watchdog, or a brood bitch, or with regard to sex, breed, behaviour, fertility, or soundness. It is taking a big risk to advertise a little puppy as "bound to become a champion". The mis-description does not have to be written, the spoken word is sufficient, provided there is a witness to it.

CRUELTY

The law lays it down that anyone convicted of cruelty to a dog may be disqualified from keeping a dog, or of obtaining a licence to keep one. The penalties for breaking such an enactment can be a fine, or imprisonment, or both at once. Any dog in the possession or an owner so convicted, whether the subject of prosecution or not, may be taken from him, if the Court so decides.

It is not necessary to say more on the vexed question of vivisection than to assure the reader that the use of animals for scientific experiment for the ultimate alleviation of disease in their fellow canines, and in mankind, is under the very strict licensed control of the government, and all such laboratories are open to inspection by the appropriate officials at any time. It is not often realized that the law relating to the treatment of animals is much more strict than that applying to human beings. You may, if you wish, consult and be treated by, a lay person. The Veterinary Surgeons Act of 1966 provides that only those registered with the Royal College of Veterinary Surgeons may diagnose and treat animal disease. The pet shop owner, or dog breeder, will be committing an offence if he prescribes for, or treats your dog, except as first aid.

There is a subtle form of cruelty unknown to few save veterinary surgeons in practice. It is the refusal of an owner of a dog to allow his pet to be put to sleep when it is the victim of an incurable and painful disease. Rather than be parted from the too-beloved creature, they (both men and women) will allow their pets to go on for weeks and months lingering to an inevitable and ever more painful termination to life. Surely the rule in such cases should invariably be that when life becomes a burden that cannot be relieved, then it is our duty to have that animal life brought to a peaceful close.

It is the responsibility of everyone who believes he has

Papillon

witnessed an act of cruelty to an animal to do all he can to bring the offender to book. Some fear the publicity involved; but in this connection it should be known that a complaint to an R.S.P.C.A. inspector in one's own locality, or by letter to the Secretary, R.S.P.C.A., 105 Jermyn Street, London, S.W.1, will always be dealt with in confidence and the complainant's name will not be divulged unless with permission.

Circuses, films, fairs and the like often employ troupes of performing dogs, or individual animals, whose training or the circumstances under which they perform, involve cruelty of greater or lesser degree. Much can be done by the public in its expressed opinions and by complaint to the police or to humane societies to lessen these occurrences.

The shutting in of dogs, and of puppies in particular, in small travelling cages, and subjecting them to long journeys by rail as well as by air transport, can be a terrifying and therefore a cruel ordeal. Don't buy dogs from afar until you are satisfied that this sort of cruelty is not likely to occur. Even the confinement of a young dog for hours at a time in a room while the family is absent from home can be an agonizing experience. Nor is the owner without blame who boards his animal out at kennels that are little better than hotbeds of disease—a situation which he knowingly accepts rather than forgo a holiday. It is your duty to inspect a kennel and to make sure that your dog will be well cared for; alternatively to arrange to leave him with a friend. These are the kinds of subtle and obscure cruelty that are so difficult to control unless people will bring them to the notice of the animal welfare societies.

Pekinese

CHAPTER IX

HOME TREATMENT

THE veterinary surgeon, like the doctor, spends quite a lot of his professional time in rescuing his patients from the results of home doctoring. Yet it is foolish to deny that there are a number of minor ailments with which the owner can cope quite successfully, either completely or at least by way of preliminary treatment, until the veterinary surgeon arrives on the scene. I suppose the trouble is that success breeds ambition; and, moreover, there is a fascination about the healing art which encourages the belief that one is more adept than is really the case, directly one or two successes with home doctoring have been achieved.

There is abundant temptation strewn in the way of the enthusiastic amateur. A study of the claims and catalogues of the patent medicine vendors can soon hypnotize the unwary into believing that there is no doggy ill that will not yield to the product in a cunning advertisement.

There is no National Health Service for dogs, and the services of a veterinary surgeon seem relatively expensive. All the same, you will be lucky if your dog does not incur some illness or accident in his life span, and such expense should be taken into account when you are deciding if you need and can afford a dog. The accumulated riches can always be given to a charity for less lucky dogs, should they not be spent. There are two rules about home treatment which will help to keep the amateur on the straight and narrow path. The first is never to treat an illness you cannot diagnose, and the second is never to treat anything for long. A condition that does not yield to home treatment in two or three days needs expert advice. I can think of nothing more galling than to take over a case only to find that for some days the patient has been saturated with a drug which either retards recovery or makes it impossible. A simple example is that of a suppurating ear. Most "Canker Powders" contain an insoluble zinc salt. This acts locally as a dryer-up of the discharge, but it also forms a cork-like plug in the ear and pens up the pus so that, in many instances, it burrows through the drum and sets up an agonizing and intractable middle-ear infection.

The second rule is never to treat a case unless you know what is wrong. Thus, to give opium to a dog exhibiting acute abdominal pain might be justified on the ground of humanity, in that it deadens pain, yet if the case is one of arrested bowel movement, the drug may well prove to be the cause of death or of a severe abdominal operation. If treatment had been withheld until a proper diagnosis was made, it could have meant all the difference between life and death.

The Animal Welfare Societies run clinics for people who really cannot afford veterinary fees. Advice will be given you, and if necessary, a voucher to help pay the fee for treatment carried out by a veterinary surgeon in private practice. To avail oneself of this concession, it will be necessary to give some details of income and employment, but in cases of true need, no animal will have to suffer neglect for want of veterinary advice.

The Small Animal side of veterinary medicine has made tremendous strides in the last twenty years. Most vets are now performing a wide range of sophisticated operations in their own surgeries, with equipment similar to that provided in human hospitals. Anaesthetic procedures have greatly improved, and high risk patients with breathing complications, like Boxers, Pugs and Pekes, have every chance of surviving a long operation without undue distress. Some veterinary hospitals have provision for keeping the dog as an in-patient until the risk of post-operative shock is past.

SPAYING

If you have no intention of breeding from a bitch, or if her breeding days are over, it makes sound commonsense to have her uterus and ovaries removed (an ovario-hysterectomy) commonly known as spaying. A lesser operation removes only the ovaries, but it is often thought wise to remove all the organs of reproduction. The fear exists that the bitch will afterwards become fat, and this may well be so, as her body is no longer subject to the stresses of heats and pregnancies, phantom or real. It is in the hands of the owner to regulate diet and exercise so that she remains fit and lean. It will probably be noticed that the coat will thicken up and become more woolly after spaying, due to continuing hormone activity.

A young bitch should be allowed one season before being spayed, so that her body achieves complete maturity. The operation is very safe, provided no uterine infection is present. The bitch will be on her feet next day, and back to full activity before the stitches are out.

Pointer

CHAPTER X

DOG DISEASES COMMUNICABLE TO MAN

RINGWORM

THIS can be a most unpleasant and intractible complaint both for the dog and for any humans involved. There are several forms; but the rat and mouse are the commonest sources. It usually starts with the formation of irritable crusts on the mouth, and in the head region, and then on the paws, where the infected parts of the head rest during sleep.

Not all the ringworms—which are a low order of spore forming vegetation resembling mushrooms in their mode of existence—are recognizable, as they generally are in the human subject by the circular patches that slowly enlarge from a centre of infection. The human being usually catches the complaint from a dog in the region of the wrists, and sometimes on the face when the obnoxious habit of kissing the dog is practised.

At the first suspicion that this unpleasant complaint exists, the dog should be taken to a veterinary surgeon, and the owner should consult his or her doctor. Some intractible types may lead to the advice that it is better to destroy the dog than to have a carrier of such a complaint about the house for months before he can be certified as free from infection.

MANGE

Sarcoptic Mange is often caught from the dog, but usually only by fair-haired people. Again, the complaint is not easily contracted, and the human hygiene will probably not be of the highest order when it is found on the owner. It is normally confined to the wrists and is easily cured. Severe cases of infection, involving the chest and limbs, have only occurred, in my experience, where the dog has shared a bed with its owner—an insanitary practice at the best of times.

WORMS

While cases of human infection with dog worm parasites have been recorded in this country, they are so rare as to make it reasonable to say that infection from the domestic pet to children in particular need not be feared. But where puppies are affected with threadworms, close contact with children is unwise until dosing has eradicated all traces of the complaint. It is most important that droppings passed after worm doses should be removed and burned if centres of infection are not to be created on lawns and in gardens. There is sound reason for not allowing children to kiss their pets, have them on their beds, or to chew grass stems.

The tapeworms, which are a common infestation once the dog has passed the puppy stage, present no direct danger to the human being, for, when voided by the dog, they have to go through the other half of their life-cycle in a grass-eating animal. In other words, if a child is found to harbour a tapeworm of the dog in his or her bowel, then it will be through eating uncooked flesh—usually rabbit—in which there are tapeworm cysts embedded in the substance of the meat.

THE DOG AS CARRIER?

The dog (as well as the cat) is often wrongly accused, even by the family doctor, of being the origin of some illness. Diptheria, influenza, scarlet fever, have all, to my knowledge, been blamed on the family pet. These diseases do not affect the dog, and he cannot bring these germs to the human being. With the exception of rabies, ringworm and mange, he keeps his diseases to himself, and only spreads them to his own tribe.

Unlike the cat, he is so strongly resistant to tuberculosis that only prolonged exposure to gross infection will set up the disease, so that to all intents and purposes he is not a T.B. carrier. That, of course, does not rule out the possibility of a dog, that has been sprayed with sputum from a lung case of human T.B., carrying the

Poodle

germs on his coat. Indeed, there are many human diseases where the discharge from nose and throat could be coughed over a dog and be temporarily carried round by him. This is one of the sound reasons why the kissing and bed-fellowship of dogs is to be discouraged, particularly with children.

But this passive carting-round of a load of germs accidentally acquired is a very different thing to becoming ill and infected with the human disease. Fortunately, when we consider the influenzas, pneumonias, dysenteries and meningitis, all of which are common afflictions of dog and man, we find that the causative germs are peculiar to each species. Were it otherwise, there would be no pets in our homes.

RABIES

This disease, transmitted by the bite of the infected dog, has been eliminated from Great Britain. This has been achieved by refusing admittance to any dog to the country until it has completed six months quarantine in approved kennels. From time to time bitter outcries occur against this method of cruelly imprisoning dogs for half a year. when, say the complainers, a simple dose of vaccine would solve the problem. So far the officials of the Ministry of Agriculture do not agree with the latter contention. The victim of a bite from a rabid dog will, in a high proportion of cases, unless treated at a Pasteur Institute before symptoms appear, suffer horribly before death occurs. And bear in mind what one dog, slipping through the quarantine regulations, can do. In 1917 a dog bit its owner's child, in England, 125 days after infection in India. Later, two men and three dogs were infected by biting before the animal was destroyed. As a further development, thirty-six dogs, four horses, and seven cattle became rabid, while eleven men and women and five children were infected and had to have preventive treatment. This single outbreak cost the country £35,000. So don't be too dogmatic about the obstinate bureaucrats in Whitehall!

A DOG SICKBAY

Despite the relative safety of nursing a sick dog, it would be foolish to ignore sick room hygiene. In a disease like distemper, many pus-forming germs gain a hold on the weak invalid, and it would be most unwise to let the copious nasal and other bodily discharges reach floors and furniture, or to let children have access to such a patient, and cuddle and kiss it. It is better to isolate and treat these discharges as possible sources of human trouble, as they are certain sources of trouble to any dogs in the neighbourhood who may contact them.

The form of jaundice brought to the dog by rats (lepto-spiral jaundice) needs care in nursing, for cases occur also in human beings. It is advisable to wear rubber gloves when handling such a disease and in giving medicine.

I would advise a similar precaution in the case of Stuttgart Disease, where the mouth, gums and tongue are invaded by a gangrene germ which, if it came into contact with broken skin or a cut, might cause blood poisoning.

Saluki

CHAPTER XI

COMMON COMPLAINTS—NURSING AND FIRST AID

IT would, of course, need a text-book to cover these topics of nursing and first aid adequately. But, after all, the intelligent amateur can for the most part recognize what is amiss, get the patient into the best environment and administer, where necessary, some simple remedy, pending the arrival of the doctor. That is as far as most of those for whom this book is designed will be wise to go without professional guidance.

Congenial Surroundings

The best nurses may be born and not made, but I have constantly observed that love and pity will go a long way to make a first-class nurse out of most unpromising material. When I am asked what is the most important requisite of a good animal nurse, I always say a knowledge of the animal's natural history.

The sick animal tends to revert to the wild state and sheds a great deal of his civilized veneer. Instincts nearly extinguished under domestication rise to the surface and may have to be pandered to in the patient. Read again the first chapter, for an intelligent nurse can deduce much from a knowledge of a species as it lives under its more primitive condition—how to regulate its diet both in time and type. Most beginners try to do too much. Many simple feverish attacks are cured by the dog starving itself and hiding away in seclusion from its fellows. Under such an affliction, it is manifestly wrong to over-fuss and ply the patient with ceaseless meals and medicine. Seclusion and limitless sleep in a temperature round about

60 degrees Fahrenheit, in a room with a window always open, to some extent conforms with the designs of Nature —which often does more than the doctor in overcoming disease. Bright lights should be shaded. The part that the colour of walls plays is not unimportant. Pale blue and primrose yellow are both peaceful colours. Kennels distempered in the latter colour will almost eliminate the tiresome barking of unhappy boarders and the colour is equally restful in the Sick Room.

Infectious Disease and Giving Medicine

Infectious disease calls for isolation. It is often the case that the nurse has to attend to both sick and healthy dogs in succession. I always advocate keeping a pair of gumboots and a mackintosh at the threshold of the Sick Room, together with a sponge and bowl of disinfectant. By sponging the sleeves and front of the mackintosh before entering and on leaving the room, as well as dipping the gumboots, infection can be localized and when the garments are removed, one can go to the in-contact or healthy animals with little fear of being a source of infection.

Open fire-places, electric and gas fires need rather special protection. I have known rooms set on fire by a delirious patient overturning an oil stove, and severe burns to occur through dogs falling into the fire-place, when weak or seized with a sudden unexpected fit, as may happen during the course of distemper.

The giving of medicine is not unduly difficult. Most dogs will allow their mouths to be handled without resentment by those they know and love. With liquid medicine, it is a mistake to try to force the mouth of a dog open. Instead, place yourself on the right of the animal and gently close the mouth with the left hand, thumb on top of the nose well above the nostrils, and the fingers in between the two branches of the lower jaw.

Even the weakest person can easily keep a dog's mouth closed, for the opening muscles of the jaw are weak, unlike the powerful closing muscles. With the jaw thus shut, insert the index finger of the right hand in the fold where upper and lower lips join. It will be found that thumb and forefinger can pull out the angle of the lips into quite a capacious pocket. If into this the medicine is poured with the head elevated a little above the horizontal, the medicine will percolate between the teeth.

Scottie

Once it is tasted, the grip of the left hand on the jaws should be somewhat relaxed to allow the liquid to flow over the tongue, when swallowing will be induced quietly and without the suffocation and fright of having it thrown into the mouth held open forcibly. Powders can be introduced by the same route, and the lips rubbed gently against the teeth and gums. This mixes the powder with the saliva, and it will not be blown out when the dog's tongue reaches it prior to swallowing.

Pills are given thus. Grasp the upper jaw only just behind the long canine teeth, pressing the lips into the mouth behind the teeth with finger and thumb. This can be done quite gently and the dog will open his mouth. I usually hold the pill or capsule between the tips of the first and second fingers of the right hand and push it well over the root of the tongue. As the fingers withdraw from the mouth, the right hand goes under the lower jaw to keep the mouth closed with the left hand which is already above and is relaxing its hold on the lips once the pill has been pushed home. Usually within a few seconds a swallow is observed, and one knows the pill has descended safely. If any of these medicine-giving tricks have been accomplished with docility on the part of the patient, a little praise and fussing, provided the operator has been gentle, will make the next time just as easy.

Sometimes the patient is vicious or the operator uncertain of the sort of welcome his efforts will get. In such a case, tie a yard of bandage into a half-knot in the middle. Place this round the jaws, with the knot beneath. Tighten and bring the ends under the ears fairly tightly and fasten with a bow at the back of the poll. A fierce dog is quite safe to handle with this simple tape muzzle, and the pocket for medicine and powders can be pulled out behind the tape as just described to receive the medicine in the same way. There may be a bit of a struggle, but if one is gentle but firm, it is surprising how most dogs will recognize the hopelessness of fighting against one who means business and will stand no nonsense. I have often noted that the second dose is given in to at once, after quite a to-do over the first, and may not even need the tape muzzle restraint any more.

The Sick Bed

The chief requisites for a sick bed are that it be reasonably soft, long enough for an exhausted patient to lie at full length, and wide enough to turn round in comfortably. A soft sack stuffed with half hay, half peat moss litter, sufficient to make a mattress four to six inches thick makes a good bed. It is advisable to pin a ground sheet of waterproof material to this where patients are likely to be incontinent. On the sheet can be laid a rug or blanket, for the patient to lie on.

When hot bottles are needed, remember that they must be checked as to their true heat some minutes after filling, before being laid under the patient. Many burns and scalds have occurred through lack of thought in this

Sealyham

respect, particularly with unconscious or semi-paralysed patients.

The floor of the sick room may well be carpeted with newspaper where the patient cannot be taken outside to relieve himself. Where a patient wets his bed through weakness, it may be necessary to lay large pads of wool under the body to absorb urine or fæces and to wash the parts of the body clean frequently that become soiled. After this, liberal dusting with talc powder is wise, or bedsores can quickly develop as a result of neglect. For cleansing, disinfecting and deodorizing the sick room, the pine disinfectants such as Dettol and Sanitas are very pleasant and non-irritating to skin surfaces with which they may come in contact.

During the profuse catarrh from the nose that is common during the course of an attack of distemper, steaming is of great help in keeping the nostrils from becoming blocked. An ordinary bronchitis kettle, to the water of which a teaspoon of Friars Balsam has been added, is as soothing an inhalant as any. Let it simmer gently for as long as necessary on the fire or on the top of a paraffin stove. There are proprietary inhalant compounds sold for human bronchitis and whooping cough, and most of them can be used with success for dogs.

Covering during Sickness

The question of wearing clothing during illness is a vexed one. On the whole, I do not recommend using coats, unless the animal is already used to them. They worry most animals and, provided the room is warm and the bed affords a blanket above and below the patient, they can be dispensed with. On the other hand, if a dog is taken out of doors in cold weather to relieve himself, it is often wise to put a coat on, particularly if it is raining. On such an occasion, the dog should have a brisk rub down with a towel on returning indoors. The pneumonia jacket, which is a sleeve-like garment applied to the chest during the course of pneumonia and made of close-fitting elastic woollen material, such as a woollen vest, may be worn for some days during the height of the disease, but this of course will be a matter for the physician to advise.

Always try to put yourself in the animal's place, if you want to succeed as a nurse. You will quickly think out ways of making an illness more bearable. Little attentions like the sponging of nostrils to clear catarrh, followed by a smear of vaseline, the washing of ill-swallowed food from the lips and cheeks, a gentle brush-up during convalescence, all help a depressed creature to perk up and decide on recovery as a worthwhile procedure.

So many text-books already exist on disease and treatment that the reader is referred to those mentioned in the last chapter as reliable sources of information on symptoms and treatment. The following notes on some common minor ailments will, it is thought, be of help to the beginner in recognizing symptoms that are mainly confined to the dog.

Skye Terrier

CHAPTER XII

NOTES ON AILMENTS

VISITS TO THE VETERINARY SURGEON

IN order to obtain the maximum benefit for your dog, and to save your own pocket from wasted visits, it is as well to marshal all the facts of the case before you go to the surgery. It is of great help to the vet if you can give a comprehensive history, and you will not be laughed at if you take some notes with you.

Suggested headings.

Age of Patient. If a puppy, where it was bought.

Inoculations. Brand used and when done. Take the inoculation certificate if possible.

Illness. When first noticed, any contributing factors such as a visit to kennels, a new diet, etc.

Diet. On what is the animal fed, how much does he have.

Drinking. Any increase in thirst. How much water is taken during the day?

Bitches. Date of last season, and pregnancies, phantom or actual.

Human Illnesses. Any unusual and undefined illness of child or adult in the household.

SAMPLES

A sample of urine is very often helpful, especially in cases of undefined general illness. It is fairly easy to get a sample by using a long handled vessel, and whipping it out from behind your back at the appropriate time. An old saucepan is suggested for dogs, a frying pan for bitches. The first visit to the garden in the morning is the best time. Not a great deal is required, a few tablespoonfuls will do. Put into a sterilized bottle, label with name, date, time and sex of patient.

Urine samples must be submitted for examination the day they are collected. Fæces samples are necessary for the diagnosis of digestive troubles, and the presence of worms. It is easy to collect a freshly produced sample on a wooden spatula and to put it into a plastic box or tin and seal with tape. Label again. If the sample has to go to a laboratory for analysis, it is best to present the sample early in the week to avoid delay in the post. In cases where poisoning is suspected, it is wise to save a sample of the substance vomited.

ACCIDENTS

Whatever the injuries, which will need professional help to elucidate, all cases of accident are in a state of shock, and should be immobilized as far as possible at once. One of the symptoms of shock is coldness, and the patient should be covered up and a warm hotwater bottle or two supplied. It is better to avoid alcoholic stimulants, as if there is internal bleeding (blanching of the gums is an indication), alcohol tends to prolong the bleeding. Sips of glucose water may be given pending the arrival of the vet. If the animal has to be lifted and moved, be very gentle, do not alter the animal's position more than necessary. A strong blanket makes a good stretcher. Any dog that has been hit by a car should be examined by a vet, even if there are no apparent signs of injury.

BLEEDING

Bleeding may be arrested by direct pressure over the wound on top of a sterile dressing. If the blood soaks through, put another pad on top rather than remove the first one. A tourniquet stops bleeding by constricting the artery supplying blood to the wound, and should only be used when bleeding cannot be controlled by other methods. Fix the tourniquet a few inches above the wound on a limb, and never leave in position for more than 15 minutes. If necessary, re-apply, a little nearer the wound, not in the same place, to save damage to underlying tissue.

BURNS

All extensive areas of burns or scalds must be seen by a veterinary surgeon at once. A burn will remain sterile for some time, as surface germs have been destroyed, so it is important not to contaminate the area. Do not apply any substance, cover with a dry sterile dressing while awaiting treatment. Keep the patient warm, give fluids, and aspirin to relieve the pain.

Small burns should have surrounding hair clipped away, and be gently cleaned with warm water to remove hair and debris. A suitable dressing is Tulle gras, covered with a sterile dressing and bandage. For a very mild burn, apply tannic acid jelly direct to the wound.

ANAL GLANDS

The dog has two glands, one each side of the anus, which sometimes become impacted through wrong diet. Signs of trouble are licking at the anus, and dragging the bottom along the ground. An abscess will form if this condition is neglected. A vet will soon evacuate the glands for you.

DISTEMPER, HARDPAD, AND CANINE VIRUS HEPATITIS

All these are virus diseases of the dog. Although all right thinking owners have their dogs immunized against such diseases, these killing diseases are still with us, and it is possible for an immunized dog to still take distemper. Symptoms are a high temperature (the normal being $101\frac{1}{2}°$ F. in the rectum), running eyes and noses, perhaps vomiting and diarrhoea, and all the signs of a very ill dog. Isolation of the patient, with disinfectant barriers round the room, is called for, and you should ask the vet to call rather than go to the surgery, to save spreading the infection.

EARS

Ears should be kept clean from puppy days, and matted hair growing within the ear should be gently removed. Ears may be gently wiped out with a little surgical spirit on cotton wool, but probes must not be used. Trouble starting in the ears is often first indicated by the head being held to one side. Any reddish brown discharge, or a bad smell coming from the ears, needs veterinary advice, as once ears become badly infected they are difficult to cure. Proprietary canker powders should never be used, as they clog the ear and prevent discharges escaping.

Deafness is sometimes congenital in white animals, the white Boxer, Bull Terrier, Dalmation and the Sealyham being typical examples. Deafness will show in these puppies at between 4 and 5 weeks, when they will not respond to sound as their fellows do. Such puppies should be put down at once, as there is no future for them. The quick response of the dog to the sound of something falling, or a vehicle approaching, is one of the best defences he has, and it takes little imagination to see how badly handicapped a dog is without hearing. The elderly animal is sometimes affected with progressive deafness, but with a lifetime of experience behind them, they can usually cope with the disability.

ECLAMPSIA

An imbalance of calcium occurring in the whelping or lactating bitch. The symptoms are panting, inability to settle with puppies, and odd behaviour, like hiding in a corner, licking the walls, etc. An immediate large dose of calcium is called for, probably by intra-venous injection. Get the vet *immediately* day or night. Immediate help reverses the condition very quickly, but convulsions and death could be the result of not recognizing the condition. For this reason, lactating bitches should never be left very long without observation.

EYES

Discharging eyes are caused by many things. In some breeds with slightly prominent eyes, dusty conditions, sand or a strong wind will cause the eyes to water.

Conjunctivitis shows itself by a redness and swelling of the eyelids, discharge of mucus, and a tendency to keep the eyes shut. It may be caused by injury, ingrowing eyelashes, or even by the vapour from over strong disinfectants used on a kennel floor. Your vet will provide the right eyedrops or ointment.

A clouding of blue across the surface of the eye is a sign of a corneal ulcer, perhaps caused by a scratch from another animal, or a rose bush. Veterinary advice should be sought at once. Never use eye drops prescribed for one condition on another, as you could do active harm and delay recovery. P.R.A. (Progressive Retinal Atrophy) is a hereditary disease, so called night blindness, as the animal stumbles into objects at dawn and dusk. There is no cure and such animals should not be bred from. Inform the breeder if this condition is positively diagnosed by a specialist.

FEET

Torn nails and cut pads bleed terribly and look worse than they are. Cotton wool soaked in Friars Balsam should be held on the foot till bleeding stops. Cut pads cannot be stitched, nor do they always unite again, but they soon cease to give pain.

Interdigital cysts are small suppurating abscesses between the toes. Mild cases can be cured by standing the foot twice daily in a basin of diluted TCP antiseptic. If cysts keep appearing, veterinary advice must be sought. Nails should be worn down, on the beach or gravel, rather than clipped. If dew claws are left on, they should be inspected periodically, to see that they are not growing round into the leg. This is particularly necessary on the very long coated breeds.

FITS

Any animal in severe pain may have a fit. Fits are complications in many diseases, or bodily disorders, and will vary in intensity from a mild head shaking and tremor, to the classic fit with racing limbs and loss of consciousness. Do not touch a dog in a fit, but guard it from danger such as falling into a fire, or a pond. As soon as possible get the dog into a darkened, quiet room, and allow no noise at all. Get the vet to come to the house as soon as possible.

When the dog is resting quietly, ice cubes may be rubbed round its head, and a dose of soluble children's aspirin given.

EPILEPSY

Some dogs have Epilepsy, which is thought to be an inherited condition. It does not usually show up until the dog is about a year old, and this may be the first indication that the breeder has mated together two animals who have Epilepsy in the carrier state, when it is undetectable. The tendency to have Epilepsy can be positively diagnosed by submitting the dog to examination by electro-encephalogram, which is quite painless and not frightening. The Epileptic dog can be treated and kept going for many years, but the breeder should always be told about the case, to avoid a repetition of the mating. Ideally, breeding stock should be screened for Epilepsy and not used if the tendency is present.

FRACTURES

Very common among breeds that play roughly, and dogs that run loose in traffic. Lift the animal carefully, keeping the injured limb uppermost. As always when an animal is in great pain, it is wise to tie a narrow piece of cloth or bandage around the muzzle and up behind the ears to tie in a bow, to prevent helpers being bitten. Even the sweetest dog may lash out under stress.

JAUNDICE

A yellow tinge to the whites of eyes, lips and unpigmented areas of skin, is the danger sign for jaundice. It could be an indication of infection by one of the two varieties of Leptospira. One of these organisms is harboured by rats and passed in their urine. Dogs who live in the country, on farms or near food stores where rats are liable to be found, should have yearly boosters of their inoculation against leptospiral jaundice.

HERNIA

Some puppies are born with a lump on the navel (umbilical hernia). This is of no consequence unless the lump begins to grow, but as the deformity is thought to be congenital, a bitch which regularly produces affected offspring should not be bred from again. A lump in the groin, in a young puppy, is an inquinal hernia, which needs surgical correction. It would not be wise to buy such a puppy from the nest.

KENNEL COUGH

Kennel cough is a virus disease, often prevalent in mid-summer and spreading quickly through boarding kennels, and over a whole area of the country. Spread is by droplet, so where dogs are gathered together, it is almost impossible to stop cross infection. The cough is harsh, dry and irritating, with a sound reminiscent of a bone being stuck in the throat, but in other ways the health is unaffected. It is thought that some dogs may be carriers. A short course of anti-biotics is indicated, to prevent secondary infections, and treatment with a linctus cough mixture, and perhaps a vapour rub on the chest. Warmth and good feeding saves the animal from getting run down, as the cough will last several weeks.

LAMENESS

Any case of front or rear leg lameness of which the cause is unknown, and which does not improve in a day or two, must be investigated by the vet. Hip Dysplasia (H.D.) is a hereditary condition showing in malformation, or disintegration of the hip joint. The condition may be quite advanced without any lameness showing. Any case positively diagnosed by X-ray should be reported to the breeder, and Stud Dogs should be submitted to the Kennel Club/B.V.A. scheme, through their veterinary surgeon, before use.

MASTITIS

Inflamed milk glands, which may occur in a lactating bitch, or in a phantom pregnancy. Hot poulticing and expelling a little milk may be tried, but if the gland does not soften up within 12 hours, get expert help.

NEPHRITIS

This is inflammation of the kidneys. It can occur as an acute infection in the younger dog, but is more commonly seen in the older animal, due to progressive deterioration of kidney function. The main sign the owner will notice is copious amounts of pale urine being passed, and a compensating increase in thirst. Vomiting and weight loss are other signs that call for professional investigation. Do not withhold water, but limit the amount given at any one time, to prevent vomiting. Try to estimate the amount of water being drunk daily, when reporting to your vet.

PARASITES

The internal parasites are worms, roundworms, hook-worms, tapeworms. Most puppies have round worms. They should be treated for them at least twice before they are sold, and it is wise to do so every six weeks for the first year. The best and most effective worm doses are obtainable from your vet.

It is particularly necessary to worm regularly where there are children in the household, and to burn the resulting excreta.

External parasites are fleas, ticks, lice and harvest mites. The best, safest and most effective dusting powder is Alugan, by Hoechst Pharmaceuticals, obtainable only through your vet. The same company make an insecticidal shampoo. Do not forget to treat the dog's bedding and collar too.

POISONING

Always a danger with such an unselective eater as the dog. Sudden vomiting and prostration must always be regarded as needing expert help at once. Common substances to look out for, as they are dangerous to dogs, are slug bait (a real killer, this), Warfarin rat poison, weedkilling sprays used along hedgerows, bait laid by gamekeepers along the edge of woodland against vermin.

Skin Conditions

Excema, Mange, and Allergical Dermatitis. Do not let a dog go on scratching an itch for long, as many simple skin conditions are made worse by a secondary infection from self-inflicted wounds. Insist on a skin scraping being taken so that the condition can be accurately diagnosed. Allergies to foods, household textiles, especially the man-made fibre carpets, and inadequately cured skin rugs, disinfectants, and washing powders are quite common in dogs. It takes patience to work through the suspect commodities. Your vet will prescribe anti-histamine tablets to subdue the itch meanwhile.

Snake Bite

Adders may be present on sandy heath lands and rocky cliffs in the summer, and dogs do get bitten. Encourage any blood to flow, to clean the wound. The progress of the poison round the body may be arrested by the use of a tourniquet. Vet needed urgently!

Stings

Wasp and bee stings are common in the dog. The first sign is usually a considerable swelling of the affected part. In the mouth and nose, a sting is dangerous. Bee stings may be removed with forceps. Very bad swelling around the mouth and eyes needs veterinary help.

Teeth

The dog has two sets of teeth, the second set coming through when the pup is aged about four months. Ears are sometimes held at peculiar angles while teething is going on. The mouth should be examined occasionally to

see that the baby teeth are falling away to let the perma-
nent set through. Special toothpaste may now be obtained for dogs, and showdogs have their teeth cleaned
regularly. Stay-at-homes may enjoy cleaning theirs on a
bone. Deposits of tartar on the gums causes bad breath.
Your vet can scale the teeth for you. Decayed teeth and
mouth abscesses usually show themselves by dribbling
from the mouth, and dis-inclination to eat. An older
dog's health often improves noticeably after bad teeth
are extracted.

UTERINE INFECTIONS

Bitches are subject to infections of the uterus. Any
abnormal discharge, opaque or coloured, between seasons,
calls for investigation as it may be a sign that pus is
building up inside the reproductive organs. After whelping there is a bloodstained discharge from the vulva for
several weeks, but it should be clean and healthy. A
black, foul smelling discharge accompanied by feverish
symptoms means that something is going wrong.

VETERINARY SPECIALISTS

As in human medicine, if you are not satisfied with the
progress being made in any condition, or if you wish to
have a diagnosis checked, you are entitled to ask for a
second opinion from a veterinary specialist. Such a
specialist may be in private practice, or may be a lecturer
at a Veterinary School. The fees charges are usually
very reasonable. In every case you must be passed on to
a consultant by your own vet, but he cannot refuse you
this privilege if you wish it.

Should you wish to change your veterinary surgeon, it
is good etiquette to do so between illnesses, and you
should not consult two practitioners about the same condition in your dog. It is becoming increasingly usual to

expect to pay cash for each surgery visit, as accounts are now only opened for big kennels.

VOMITING AND DIARRHOEA

A dog vomits easily, and his intestines are very sensitive to change in diet. Any changes should take place very gradually, adding a tablespoonful of the new substance each day until a complete change is made. Often a new food may take the blame for "turning him out", when it is just that his system has not adjusted to it. Liver in particular has this effect on some dogs.

A bitch will often vomit partly digested food for her puppies at weaning time, sometimes hours after she has taken it. This is messy, and annoying, but a perfectly natural process.

Diarrhoea can be a symptom of many internal disturbances. If the animal appears otherwise well, withhold food for a day, giving only glucose and boiled water. If the situation is improving after 24 hours, give very small quantities of cooked white fish and plain boiled rice six times a day, to get the digestion going again. Dogs will often cause themselves an upset such as this by eating cow and horse manure, or decomposing refuse. Blood-stained diarrhoea or extreme looseness, accompanied by vomiting and prostration require veterinary help quickly. Keep the patient warm meanwhile. Frequent bouts of explosive diarrhoea may mean colitis, a hereditary disease in some breeds. Veterinary advice is needed. Diarrhoea in young puppies pulls them down very quickly, and should never be neglected. Expert diagnosis is needed, as it may have so many causes.

EUTHANASIA

Putting to Sleep. The greatest mercy we can give a dog who is too old and ill to enjoy life, or who has become, through neglect or ill-treatment, impossible to have as a pet in the home. Dogs with major defects of temperament do occur, even in the easiest breeds, and such dogs are not acceptable for family life. The risk that they might one day attack is too great to be borne. There is sometimes a temptation to offer such a dog as a guard dog, or even, worst of all, to a kennels for breeding. We should have the courage to decide that the treacherous, bad-tempered or over-possessive dog has no place in the world. Never, never, take a dog, be it an old beloved pet or a problem dog, and hand it in to the surgery "to be put down" so that its last minutes are spent with apprehension among strangers. Euthanasia by a veterinary surgeon is completely peaceful and untraumatic, but if the relationship with your pet has meant anything to you, you owe it to him to be the last face he sees, the last voice he hears, before he slips into the unconsciousness from which there is no waking.

Smooth Haired Fox Terrier

CHAPTER XIII

MISCELLANEOUS INFORMATION

THE KENNEL CLUB. 1 Clarges St., Piccadilly, London, W.1. For all information appertaining to shows, registration of kennels and dogs, transfer of ownership.

R.S.P.C.A. Headquarters at Manor House, Horsham, Sussex. Maintains clinics under veterinary care for the animals of poor people in all principal cities and towns. Uniformed inspectors deal with complaints of cruelty from the public. The address of the local inspector can be got from any police station. Branches also in Scotland and Ireland.

NATIONAL CANINE DEFENCE LEAGUE. 10, Seymour St., Portman Sq., London, W.1. This charity has kennels in several parts of the country where sanctuary is given to stray and abandoned dogs. They find homes for dogs which have been discarded as pets or whose owners have died or taken ill. Dogs that cannot be found homes are maintained for life.

They provide treatment free through their own clinics for needy pet owners, and they have a mobile clinic which is famous for its work in needy areas.

Help is given to old age pensioners in the payment of their dog licences each year, enabling them to retain the companionship of their dogs without hardship. Any pet owner can get a pet's identification disc through the N.C.D.L., who will send details of this service on request.

They also welcome requests for details of their postal dog training course for owners, which can be undertaken at home. All these and other services such as Public Liability Insurance are available to subscribing members of the N.C.D.L.; subscriptions can be either on an annual or life membership basis, and subscription income of course forms one of the mainstays of this organization's worthwhile work. Details from the above address.

NATIONAL DOG OWNERS ASSOC. Green Castle, Goudhurst, Kent. Third party insurance cover for members' dogs (£100,000 maximum). Residential Trainers Course. Bi-monthly magazine.

THE ANIMAL HEALTH TRUST. 24 Portland Place, London, W.1. This is the only charitable institution in the

St. Bernard

U.K. which seeks to investigate and alleviate disease in animals. Founded by the late Dr. W. R. Wooldridge, C.B.E., F.R.C.V.S., the Trust grants post-graduate training scholarships, as well as carrying out research programmes at its own centres. At the Small Animal Centre at Lanwades Park, work is in progress on leukaemia in the dog and cat, and mammary cancers in the bitch.

All this work depends on voluntary contributions from those who have the welfare of the dog at heart.

BATTERSEA DOGS HOME. 4 Battersea Park Rd., S.W.8. Collects and disposes of unwanted dogs.

THE BLUE CROSS. The Animal Hospital, Hugh St., S.W.1.

PEOPLE'S DISPENSARY FOR SICK ANIMALS. High St., Dorking, Surrey.

QUARANTINE REGULATIONS for dogs entering and leaving the country, Ministry of Agriculture & Fisheries, Hook Rise, Tolworth, Surrey.

DOG PHOTOGRAPHERS. Angel Photographic, Angela Cavill, 21, Post Horn Lane, Forest Row, Sussex. Phone: Forest Row 3163.
Miss Anne Roslin-Williams, The White House, Clifton, Sevenstoke, Worcs. Phone: Sevenstoke 384.

TRANSPORT OF DOGS. Ryslip Livestock Shipping, Binfield Park, Bracknell, Berks.
Pedigree Air Services, P.O. Box 52, Braywick House, Braywick Rd., Maidenhead, Berks.

KENNEL STATIONERY. L. & E. Elbourne, 1, Olave Close, Lee-on-Solent, Hants.

KENNELS. E. F. Hare & Sons Ltd., Upper Mills Industrial Estate, Bristol Rd., Stonehouse, Glos.

FOODS. Biscuit. 100% Wheatmeal. Laughing Dog Biscuit, Roberts & Co. (Dunchurch) Ltd., Dunchurch, Rugby.
Tinned Meats. Pedigree Petfoods. Spratts Patent Ltd. Complete Air-Dry Diets. Purina. Jenks Bros. Foods, 21, The Arcade, The Octagon, High Wycombe, Bucks. Wuffitmix. B. Dugdale & Sons, Waterloo Cornmill, Clitheroe, Lancs. Bone Meal. W. & J. Dunlop & Co., Ltd., 18 Bank St., Dumfries.

INSURANCE OF DOGS. Canine Insurance Association, Calia House, 24/26 Spring St., Paddington, W.1.

BOOKS. *Practical Dog Breeding and Genetics*, by Eleanor Frankling. Published by Popular Dogs.

The Care of the Family Puppy, by Robert C. White, M.R.C.V.S. Published by Popular Dogs.

Dogs and How to Breed Them, by Hilary Harmar. Published by John Gifford.

Anatomy of the Dog, by Dr. R. N. Smith, PH.D., D.SC., F.R.C.V.S. Published by Quartilles.

The Dog Directory. Published annually by Joe Cartledge, Binfield Park, Bracknell, Berks.

A comprehensive guide to the breeders who can supply you with a puppy at the present time. Also up to date list of training clubs, boarding kennels, trimming and grooming experts. Addresses of Secretaries of Breed Clubs, who can give you information about the breed, social activities for members, magazines etc.

DOG NEWSPAPERS. Published weekly.

Dog World. 32 New Street, Ashford, Kent.

Our Dogs. Oxford Road Station Approach, Manchester, 1.

Welsh Springer Spaniel

INDEX

alsation, 37

ALL UNIFORM WITH THIS BOOK

The Right Way to

Keep Pet Fish

by REGINALD DUTTA, B.A., F.Z.S.

This book is invaluable to those who have taken up or are about to take up the ever-increasing art of fish-keeping. An informative and instructive guide covering everything for the Aquarium, Coldwater or Tropical and the Outdoor Pond. Veterinary Record: '. . . can be recommended to the rapidly-increasing number of aquarists. . . . practical and readable.'

The Right Way to

Keep Hamsters

by ROY ROBINSON

An ideal and accurate guide for both child and adult on the proper way to rear and care for these creatures. As a member of the Institute of Biology, Roy Robinson is supremely well-qualified to write on this subject. He has been breeding hamsters and other rodents for about 20 years.

ELLIOT RIGHT WAY BOOKS, KINGSWOOD, SURREY, U.K.

PAPERFRONTS

Ford Escort Repairs

The Slimming Secret

Crosswords for the Enthusiast

Bridge – Quiz from a New Angle

Very Advanced Driving

Deep Freeze Secrets

The Right Way to Play Chess

Antique Furniture Expl. & Illust.

Progressive Brain-Teasing Quizzes

Learning to Drive in Pictures

Car Doctor A–Z

More Golf Secrets

Home Medical Encyclopedia

Sunshine Phrase Books in French, Spanish, Italian and German

All uniform with this book

ELLIOT RIGHT WAY BOOKS,
KINGSWOOD, SURREY, U.K.

PAPERFRONTS